THE PERFUME OF LIFE · BOOK ONE

The Perfume of Life

BOOK ONE
SENSES AND CORRESPONDENCES

Saffron and I set off to Mexico.

A.S. REISFIELD

Ediciones Vanguardistas

SAN MIGUEL DE ALLENDE

MEXICO

The Perfume of Life: Book One

ISBN: 978-0-9975341-0-8

Ediciones Vanguardistas
San Miguel de Allende, Mexico

The Perfume of Life trilogy is
One: Senses, Two: Essences, and Three: Confidences

For news about events related to the book,
see the website at www.theperfumeoflife.com

I would like to express my thanks to Suzanne Noguere for copyediting
and proofreading the three books of the trilogy, Elizabeth Watt for the
cover photos, Nisha Ferguson for the cover lettering, Lander Rodriguez
for the cover design and typesetting, and Erika Corral for additional
language editing.

Perfumes of Entry

We join this tale as three perfumers are being pressed to detail why certain provisions of their trade appear to be wanting, like comfort or clarity or assurance that meaning exists in the world, or affirmation that it doesn't exist, or assertion of order in the universe or declaration of disorder or whatever other decree may be on some wish-list or must-have list...

There's a lot more to this story (or chemical fairytale, a fantasy that bears on perfumery) but after several years I tired of working on it. I decided that it was a big mistake, so I stopped.

It appears that the three will now be compelled to learn a hard lesson (an understatement) about certain human needs...

And I've been upset at myself for wasting so much time with this contrived manner of narration. And my poor judgment drained my confidence for a period.

Saffron remains seated during the reproach, Tulip tries to ignore the assailing crowd, Licorice attempts to walk away, each hoping that the hecklers will eventually empty themselves of enmity, but the opposite effect takes hold...

Well, this writing has finally taken a turn, as I've shifted to favor an entirely different type of account, a chronicle of sessions, studies that take up critical questions, something like a journal of polemical appeals and chemical investigations. The respective entries will be sorted into three books, arranged loosely to reflect the chronology by which the principal characters—Saffron, Tulíp, and Licorice—arrive to join the proceedings here in Mexico. Altogether the series of volumes may be regarded as a record of our work and our recent experiences (granted, owing to certain developments that I'll detail later, the fate of the salons, the classes, our residence, everything, is presently not clear).

All right, that'll be the extent of prefacing for now, except to establish, before moving on to start with Book One, that the subject of our inquiry is the matter of perfume, to be construed in the broadest sense of the term. And also, to bring home the idea that this writing is being submitted as both a serial novel and a study guide. At this time, we're designating the trilogy of books by the working title *The Perfume of Life*.

Contents

CONTENTS

CONTENTS

Perfumes of Portent

"Let's begin?"

Allow me just this interruption to apologize for my repeated warnings here (yes, it seems heavy-handed, I'm sorry for that—really, not so sorry, because it calls for reminding, over and over, the awareness we draw from our scentful subjects, the vaporous voicings, the fragrant agents of Creation) that humanity is laying siege to Life, and we're not going along, we're not following.

"Latecomers, please find your seats."

That's to say that we won't abide all the reducing by the Nature-abusing magi of cosmological musing and mathematical proving. We're refusing.

"Welcome, salonists, on behalf of your Salonnier—"

The posited idea that physics explains chemistry which explains biology which explains psychology which explains philosophy, during its passage to turn into a truth, became confused in regard to chemistry, and then completely disoriented in the matter of biology. So it remains just an idea, foreign to our experience.

"He'll be your neovitalist tour guide for the evening—"

There's a pathway of nerves and hormones that runs from your *nariz* to your brain and then to your genitals by way of your pituitary, hence we refer to the naso-hypothalamic-hypophyseal-gonadal bridge ... like the sound of it?

"To provide annotation on behalf of Creation—"

I have on my mind the denial of Life, and the design of such a drive, that is, the mechanisms applied in order to deprive the wild and alive, to put down aliveness and even lifelikeness, and the urgent rightness of our beholding this crisis unfolding.

"As we survey the intensifying technological mugging of Life."

We have this vial, supposed secret chemistry of Creation. We won't make much of it since a planned event would be interpreted as a publicity stunt.

"I assist with the planning and presentation."

The rarest most peculiar intricacy indicates the secret chemistry. The most aberrant idiosyncrasy indicates the secret chemistry. The most freakish teratism indicates the secret chemistry. The deviant in you understands it. What is it?

"So are we set to get this ritual going?"

It shows an orange tint when held up to sunlight. It fluoresces blue in moonlight. And, yes, the chemical profile has been evaluated with reports by three different analytical labs, raising more questions than answering, no matter.

"Testing blotters are freshly imbued and ready for passing."

Shortly we'll discuss the masterful Perfume Industry marketing campaigns: why Brazilians choose to poison themselves with fruity fragrances, while Arabs opt to court death by the route of oriental and musky volatile accords, as Russians are inclined toward heavy and rich aromatic toxicants, yet Chinese prefer suicidal play with light and airy odorful etherealizations.

"Then it's time to provide tonight's preambulary affirmation?"

Let's see if I have this right: we're not accepting of how life ends, so we set about with methods of evasion, not comfortable with what we know, so we try to change the equation, not pleased with how it goes, so we try to destroy Creation? to somehow move beyond Life? meaning that we're needing to somehow tip the balance of being, as we're not conceding to the limits of organic experience. The historic fate of perfume reveals the sad spectacle.

"And now, let's have our panel members introduce themselves?"

Just one more interruption, however untimely, to relay an account of Sierra Leonean rebel brutality, as it bears on our inquiry, you'll see. It's about how this family, a mother who was an amputee and her two adolescent daughters, were tied to a tree, and firewood and rifles were shoved up into the three. The point being that, notwithstanding the agony, they were among the fortunate that day.

Perfumes of Carriage

"...whoosh, pass the message—the volatile monoterpene sabinene, coming from foliage of grapefruit and mandarin trees in Italy, fleeing the fluid petitgrain oil of distillation, issues herby and woody while still spicy and oily though weedy yet warmly seedy odor traces to metabolite stores of thousands of species of plants (hundreds recorded) including marjoram cypress juniper tarragon and basil, and in trace concentrations joining with a myriad more, really it's easier to list natural perfumes absent this molecule, which additionally serves pheromonal and defensive interests of swallowtails and birch bugs and bark borers, and intermingles among vapors of Sri Lankan nutmeg plants with—psst, pass the message—"

We do our best but it's hard, sure, to summon a fitting response to the stealthy sweeping assault on things materially meaningful, meaning things sensible and Earthly, meaning genuinely worthy in the sense of being genuine and Earthbound, to identify the gathering yet morphing monstrosity, a kind of global super-mechanism, how even to reference this juggernaut, to sort through all the commentary, each party with its pet explanation and favored interpretation, often catchall or all-encompassing, hominid evolution or historic imperialism or Renaissance science or central banking, a cyber-industrial complex of data technologies managing information everywhere, some secret cabal or society, hegemonic corporate cartels like that of big oil, a demonic worldview or brutish social order or malignant malady of civilization—

"... whoosh, pass the message—the psychoactive phenylpropene myristicin, which lends to boundary layer gasses of dill and nutmeg fruit (including the involucrum, mace) some softly glowing balsamic elements rendered zestful by a peppery facet, and also interacts by accommodation with agglomerations of aroma compounds emitted by European populations of curly-leaf parsley, which include—psst, pass the message—"

... military or political or theological strategies to extend reaches of influence, to pacify and seduce, convert and reduce, to control one way or another, how shall we name it, this aggregate entity that depreciates Living Nature, this amorphous thing that is somehow appointed to tear at the fabric of Life on Earth, to administer the modern-day unraveling, while funneling wealth to beneficiaries, it's self-perpetuating and auto-escalating, but it persists as more than a pyramid of power, too slowly we come to make out its biophobic core and central neomanic thrust, the driving recklessly to dominate all that's organic, all that's breathing, any alive being, whatever is vital and wild, including the wild within us, any pumping heart or proliferating tissue or active mind, any old-growth forest or barrier island, any tropical floodplain or alpine flora, any garden terrace or desert fauna—

"... whoosh, pass the message—the monoterpene beta-phellandrene, which elicits a taste of turpentine-soaked mint leaves whereas a sense of apiaceous seasoning is also perceived, a principle distributed generously among vascular plants and especially contributed along the line of umbellifers such as lovage and dill and angelica, is borrowed by cherry fruit flies and blackberry aphids and pine engravers for their communications, and involved with stands of anacard pepper trees, which dispatch scentful effluvial fruit cocktails incorporating—psst, pass the message—"

...still we should characterize this universalizing phenomenon that blankets and infects and blasts apart, like a relentless powered automaton, overwhelming any opposition, requiring only occasional fueling and tinkering by appointees, a rivet here, a nut there, bearings are greased, a belt frays, a dowel cracks, on the other side we find a futile neo-Luddite flare-up here, a pointless attempt to sabotage there, the pockets of resistance offering no hope, akin to heterogeneous and discombobulated Davids, going against a menacing planetary Goliath...

"...whoosh, pass the message—the sesquiterpene alcohol viridiflorol, which specializes in imparting volatile touches of tropical unripe fruits as well as a vaguely minty maybe but mainly faintly floral mellifluousness found especially among perfumes wafting around communities comprising cistus or manuka or cajuput or niaouli or dalmatian sage, counting also emanations from terpene-rich Somali olibanum where it teams with other thuriferous components to make incense-themed perfume—muah, pass the message—"

Perfumes of Narration

"So is the aim of the matter to save or to savor the fate or the flavor of Living Nature?"

Okay, I'm ready now, to try and explain our figuring.

The story of the universe—the book of the universe—is written in the language of numbers, mathematics, equations and proofs and theorems. We've no time for and not much interest in numbers.

Stories of the heart—the book of love—are written in the language of music, a longtime passion of mine, but presently we're trying to readjust the disposition of our radar.

The story concerning humanity on Earth—the book of people and planet—is written in the language of light, our origins and history best recounted by frames of color, such visual creatures we are. Chapters of this book may provide compelling accounts of some other forms of Life too.

Stories concerning our existential longing for beauty and meaning—the book of human wonder—are written in the language of language, poetry and prose. A great book for sure, but we're lately trying to redirect the angles of our antennae.

"...and from the uteruses of cows flew out birds who opened their beaks to let out snakes from whose eyes emerged swarms of bees who coalesced around a hive that grew into moss from whose strobili sprang monkeys..."

Because stories concerning Nature—the book of Life—are written in the language of volatile molecules, metabolites of organic beings that live in our environments presently and through all history—that's the language of perfume.

Perfumes of Aspect

"It's not fixation, it's acknowledgment," Saffron advertises her arrival.

Now ... I should preface the presentation following with a bit about myself, but I think I'll refrain from that kind of introduction, except to say that I'm a perfumer, albeit I've never yet made any perfume to completion. Still I'm prone to show off my latest study or new accord, would-be components of finished fragrant compositions, though I'm not adept at perceiving or distinguishing scents, to the contrary, for me it's the idea, I get hung up, absorbed by imaginative association, always mulling over.

"Sorry to inform you, Salonnier, with this unsolicited appraisal, but your blends of botanical extracts bear the same stamp of crudeness as your paintings and recordings, reflecting the hand of a composer with discipline lacking and a repertoire excessively personal."

And I'm interested in the nature of artistic composition, and the frequently visiting question about means and ends and media of art, that is, which media best befit the furthering of which ends—makes sense?

"You are chronicling our experiences?"

I'll take that question as a prompt to offer a limited exposition for the benefit of readers, allowing that later I might present more than a minimal setup. But this is just to set the stage, to issue notice that I'll be depicting a kind of prodigy who has been assisting me to preside over a series of aroma salons and related sessions. I'm not given much to describe or extol, nor to chart or explore my relationships with women (even if I understood these better), can't even summarize my feelings properly, but, yes, I'm referring to Saffron, my assistant. And soon I'll also be introducing two other helpmates, each in turn provocative (in a favorable way), Tulíp and Licorice.

"The central theme is that we are groundbreakers in the matter of perfume."

I would provide a rough account of the narrative but I'm presently writing and can't foretell all the circumstances ahead. Yet I can reveal that the proceedings begin just prior to our moving the perfume panel operation to high montane middle Mexico, which is where most of the exercises take place, where vapors readily cut loose from their sources, owing to the elevation in the clouds, and where there is cultural engrossment with the idea of death, which bears on our inquiry into the phenomenon of Life.

"The critical feature is that we are pioneers of this kind of program."

Whereas we might not be alone, still we surely go further, in considering that volatile fragrant metabolites of Nature constitute collectively the fundamental currency of information among the living, that they are agents common by their heritage to all Life, that they are drawn to Life, with affinity to living tissue, that they are elemental messaging transmissions of Life, molecular emissaries that uniquely express Life, authentic manifestations of Life. And it follows that by beholding the previously veiled story that is faithfully channelled by perfume, we best come to understand the epical history and present state of Life on Earth.

"The crucial point is that the drama is crystallized as chemistry."

To administer the plant perfume salons, our compasses are calibrated toward whatever directions our studies lead, concerning the nature of Life and aliveness. (I admit to some misgivings, as we've been lured to track coveted grails, things beyond our sovereign competence, like the ordering principles or secret ciphers of Creation, laws of Nature, all that.) Nonetheless, by our practice we're eventually guided to view the story of stories, the all-out offensive against organic complexity, against the particularities of Life. (And I don't agree that any of this is blustery to proclaim.)

"The heart of the matter is that our vaporous subjects are prone to being reverse-engineered and recast, atomized assayed and appropriated, manipulated muddied and made over."

The assault is tricky to pin down, described variously by commentators viewing from different angles, through different filters. But we have an advantage, best seat in the house, unobstructed field of vision—we try to downplay abstract cerebral formulations and study our subjects squarely—flowers soils seeds leaves rivers fruits bugs and beasts, their communications vital and pressing—perfume! (In consideration of all beings wild and free yet vulnerable and screaming silently, a sense of urgency is here conveyed with intention.)

"The driving idea, though our unlikely endeavor may go against the odds, is to influence in some way the crisis unfolding, to make a difference."

Perfumes of Warning

It's odd, yes, the way perfumers provoke in me, I'm afraid to confess, a steeping animus.

"These *mouillettes* are ready and dripping, and we have enough samples of clove oil here to warrant a short panel review, so let's get dipping," Saffron announces.

Perfumers are recklessly committed to a world of their own designing. Perfumers have an especially twisted addiction to control. Perfumers thrive within demoralizing corporate economies. Perfumers practice exercises for accruing influence. Perfumers operate under cover of Chemical Industry power. Perfumers turn permission granted into compulsive pursuance. Perfumers are heedless that synthetic molecules they introduce show up in breast milk of nursing mothers. Perfumers are best friends with plastics and pesticides.

"*El clavo*," the salonists in attendance take turns salonizing, "not much is needed of this convincing Zanzibarian stem oil to experience its aromatic statement—the sensation is like an even headier version of wet kretek clove cigarettes—exhales pales of old island rum, bales of Christmas potpourri, and trails leading to the secret Coca-Cola recipe?—note the touches of cassia and cardamon, allspice and agrumen—this selection emerges like a eugenol incendiary, striking chords that are harsher and cruder and woodier than its sibling leaf and bud extracts—the inducive effusion results from the emissive diffusion and produces a sensory confusion by reason of its uncommon action on the sense of olfaction—"

Perfumers trivialize the harmful effects of their fragrances on organic communities. Perfumers cynically lay siege to wild plants under the pretense of botanical art. Perfumers denigrate the Natural World by patenting genuine forms of Life. Perfumers chase down beings that are wild and free. Perfumers prey on the most vulnerable of organisms and species. Perfumers defraud indigenous societies by their bioprospecting. Perfumers further the decline of thriving seas and fresh breezes and vital foods and sexual feelings.

"...this next is a Malagasy leaf oil, more dry and transparent—summoning recollections of odorful impressions of toasted bread and similar cinnamic fractions from chemical reactions amounting to maillard browning—clove with wintergreen is a good base for root beer?—methyl salicylate, the remindful medicinal principle of wintergreen (due to its commanding concentration in that distillate), makes a trace showing among volatiles that waft from clove foliage—and eugenol, the pronounced and pervading spicy core constituent derived from clove trees, gives a character-determining display among headspace components discharging from carnation flowers—(and makes guest metabolic appearances throughout the kingdoms of Life)—"

Perfumers commoditize Creation. Perfumers reduce and corrupt our experience of authentic Nature. Perfumers champion a promiscuous program to remake fragrant Life. Perfumers promote aesthetic atrophy. Perfumers feign formulating with plant extracts as they endorse biotic cleansing. Perfumers advance by disregarding notions of limits. Perfumers are in the business of making projectile instruments of aggression. Perfumers thus embrace and encourage aggressive culture. Perfumers deal in dominance and delusion.

"Clearly, perfumers steal food from starving children when no one is looking."

Worse, perfumers violate the integrity of Living Nature. Perfumers despoil our biological heritage of immense natural variety. Perfumers stimulate the accelerating deterioration of local ecologies around the planet. Perfumers are faithfully infatuated with technological wonders. Perfumers sustain a self-congratulating trust in their own judgment. Perfumers suffer from delusional thinking. Perfumers apply their disengaged imaginations to reengineer our environments. Perfumers plunge ahead. Perfumers fly blind.

"...aroma elements (infochemical couriers of content aka scent) issued by this next sample reflect features we associate with nutmeg and vanilla, ylang-ylang and cola, this being an American distillation of Sri-Lankan-harvested clove buds—there's a release of a slight vinous installment, agreed?—and an implied dusty or musty cresylic nuance on the side or the underside—an expression of early ethereal juiciness gives way to a tarrying woody flourish, then the resurrection of phenolic smoke—"

"Who will explain why the middle cuts of a wormwood distillation are frequently considered clove-like?"

Perfumers replace gardening with photos of gardens. Perfumers replace singing with systems of notation. Perfumers replace sensual sentiments with detached poetry, then replace poetry with mission statements.

"…the designation of fruitiness, an apt attributive perhaps, but not in the sense of a reference to actual fruits, rather more like the fragrant elicitation of certain fresh-splashing terpenoid and aldehyde and ester compounds as they lift off from flowers such as jasmine and marigold, mimosa and carnation—in particular, the lightest fraction of clove bud oil is often inferred to be inimitably albeit modestly fruity (in a clovey way)—that aspect is scentingly contributed by methyl n-amyl ketone (which turns up to suggest spearmint in another context)—traces of benzaldehyde are in there too—"

Perfumers replace the experience of love with promotional campaigns about love. Perfumers replace flirting and playing and kissing with botox and facelifts. Perfumers replace male libidinal excitement with vacuum penile pumps.

"…the Indonesian bud oil emits molecular morsels like oozing emanations which radiate the vibrations we associate with rich warm caramelic butter and cream—initially it shows a shade of banana then malty vanillin then midway a urine note materializes maybe or it might be a volatile tickle of some beaver or similar titillating secretion—with resonant vapors of incense and spices amidst the mix that persist to exist upon fading to an abyss while we reminisce—"

This is just to name a few warnings about perfumers. I'll name their names too, you'll see. It appears that no one else is willing.

Perfumes of Projection

"Whatever deserves our love, it's under assault."

Saffron, ready to relocate to a house on a rock in a spot beside a draw around a hill on the side of a mountain that adjoins a jagged range bordering the Central Mexico altiplano? Our arrival is anticipated.

The backstory of stories is the wild open realm of Living Nature, of elaborate complexity founded and compounded by countless ecological interactions over myriad millennia, finally bequeathing the fluid hodgepodge of Earthly diversity and the prolific aimless intricacy of Life. Our plotline chronicles how natural history is unheeded and endemic floras are degraded, how natural resources are depleted and faunas raided, how Nature is de-Natured as Life is negated.

"Let's see if I have this right," she looks up from her notes, as if auditioning for a theatric role—

Our featured story of stories involves the loose disarray and backdrop bouquet of biotic communities, the colorful and complicated fabric of fragrance, the untidy diffusion of metabolic transmissions that hold latent meaning and implied designs, that harbor subtle symbols and evocative signs, and that may stir feelings, spark ideas and ignite ideals.

We help to make sense of what's issued, to engage with what's presented.

"...it's hard finding ways back to the experience of aromatic expression, the primary mode of organic connection, considering our impoverished appreciation of Creation, in the course of our daily stifling contact with Earth-incongruous commodities of scent, developed by committees of (you name them) venturesome enterprisers in mass and power perfumery—"

(she stops to take a breath)

"...and the wide-scale saturation bombardment by the context-disregarding ecology-deriding and Life-disdaining, of our progressively denuded environments with caustic test-tube innovations purposed to meet xenobiotic specifications, under cover of abstruse layers of misleading maxims and deceiving depictions of odorous formulations by guileful perfumers and their prevaricating posses—"

(again she breathes and continues)

"...currencies of light and sound too, like fragrance, are subjects of abstract theorizing and sinister manipulation and industrial appropriation, but campaigns to co-opt painting and music by reductionist machineries are never complete victories as there are always a few survivors among the cultural wreckage finding their way back to simple artfulness with unadorned pigments and tones—"

(she takes a last deep breath)

"...but aromatic materials are of a different order, posing different challenges."

Nice, Saffron. I'm lucky to have your assistance by the way you deliver so faithfully our message agreed upon.

"Dust be diamonds, water be wine, happy time."

Perfumes of Appeal
(Patchouli)

(I tap *clink-clink* to a wine glass.)

Greetings, and so on . . . all that. Please find your seats around our fabled table, as tonight's testing blotters are all but labeled, so the perfume salon will begin in a minute, and don't worry, we'll commit to limit the preambulary sharing, we promise, except to note that—

"Olfactive indications of ripe berries in a moist meadow connote cured tobacco of a balsamic cigar or dry cinnamon deposited in heavy dirt like black soil turned over dank leaves near an old barnyard where a friendly goat chews on a soaked cloth next to a worn saddle that evokes a soggy sponge or rooty earth plus a bitter spice in a dark basement bordering a mucky swamp colonized by aromatic moss growing in warm mud within a damp forest—what, these are sensorial impressions of a single sample of patchouli essential oil?"

. . . that the wealthy and privileged rarely have to smell the stench of decomposing bodies.

"The forceful feral and erotic mysterious sensual and

chameleonic emanations reference sensations of ambergris wine furniture cigarettes henna salt and cedarwood."

In 1915, Armenians were deported from their homes in what is now Turkey. Over a million traveling in caravans were raped and beaten with clubs and hammers.

In 1937 Nanking, tens of thousands of women were gang-raped by Japanese soldiers over a three-week period. Men were made to rape their daughters and sons their mothers. From door to door, even young children were dragged away to be abused, mutilated and murdered, over a thousand a day.

"Well, first of all, patchouli is cultivated and distilled primarily in Indonesia," Saffron says.

Indonesian militia just a few decades ago stayed busy torturing East Timorese, with steel poles shoved down their throats and electric shocks to their genitals. The victims were hung by chains and forced to eat dirt, babies smashed against rocks, residents burned and raped and starved until around two hundred thousand were murdered.

"The vaporous construction begins with early herby ethereal scouts off the *mouillette* which pave the way for a deep vinic structural transmission succeeded by a slowly evolving balsamic underlayer and a woody character in the hereafter."

The living plants? are not given to dispatch any of the distinguishing patchouli fragrant principles, since leaf glandular hairs physically resist setting the volatiles free.

"Awaiting our review are an imposing number of infochemical emissions: red and brown, light and dark, amber organic conventional and filtered, several vintages … no time."

But it happens that leaves are induced to release the scentful metabolites to steam after a controlled cultural protocol of limited drying and interrupted fermentation designed to compromise the integrity of cell walls, in this way readying the characteristic patchouli perfume for its abduction.

"Insofar as iron stills are customarily used still, this traditional manner of distillment turns out what are known as village oils, which pick up iron and are thus prone to turn darker, and so are sometimes treated to become lighter, touched up to tone down the brown."

And producers? have developed specialties such as molecular distillates, various selections and filtrates of refinement, materials of so-called sophistication, supercritical and other fractional extracts ... altogether adding to the overall diversity of products traded.

"The double-distillate, being twice distilled, displays a modulated astringency dually instilled, and the sensory profile is smoother than silk."

Over time, sesquiterpenes oxidize and eventually polymerize, to form long-chain resins ... which enhance the impressions?— it's true, aging oils don't decay, rather they're on their way to developing an improved bouquet.

"The five-year aged imparts a lasting rich ambience of herbaceous radiance in small installments—from these sludgy flourishes, which are like base tones or bass notes, one makes out a redolent regard to robust bottomland that lingers in the nare hairs—the hint of mint is a tacit facet—the effluvium elicits an associative reaction like a recollection of chalky sun-baked ground, after a rainstorm."

Actually, odor molecules circulating in the air originate from soil microorganisms, and adhere in what appears like a film to clay particles that constitute everyday dust on any given ground, and are set loose on any given day by rain, hence the unmistakeable discharge of a fungal fresh vegetal perfume of wet earth.

The notes are brown and green, much as hues may be soft and rounded yet penetrating. In Septimus Piesse's system of scent transcribed to musical notation, patchouli is a bass clef C3, does that sound right? In any case, we're faced with a synesthetic soup of suggestions.

"From Hainan Province, the portrayal of the oil belongs in the domain of the open drain, or maybe that's animal funkiness meaning muskiness which I'm confusing with fustiness meaning dustiness?—Chinese distillations are prone toward dirtiness—the Sumatran is a raw rendering, more bitter and smoky around the edges—and revealed to contain iron by its metallic kick?—the Indonesian oils tend toward earthiness—the iron-free is next, it projects an adobe brick construction which fades to a foundation that's more musty than foxy (perhaps the leaves dried too slowly, or fermented for too long?)—the Philippinan greets our senses with aromatic cocoa powder—the Indian gushes gases concentrated of patchoulol, giving a finer, more reserved adaptation—the European oils are disposed toward fruitiness."

Whereas yes, patchouli alcohol is a majority constituent, another sesquiterpene alcohol, norpatchoulenol, has a negligible presence yet influences a greater proportion of the composite fragrance. This latter sesquiterpenoid is a minority component by measure of mass but not of organolepsis.

"The absolute exhibits an elegant complex core of composting fruit surrounded by an elaborate envelope of mire (solvent extraction, whether with hexane or carbon dioxide, eliminates the need for hot processing, which allows for the preservation of labile compounds and thus the provision of a broader range of chemical messages).”

And in another context, though it may be off topic, and you may not care, the ligneous earthy camphor-splashed patchouli alcohol combines into an accord with the element of valeric cheesiness, and you may not care about where, but that would be among volatiles riding the Himalayan air, those extricating from spikenard plants over there.

“Really, a homework assignment? to list all the variables that influence oil quality?—let's see ... soil type, geographic region, farming practices, weather, genetic stock, plant parts and growth stage when harvested, the drying, fermenting, distillation parameters, aging of the distillate, and subsequent manipulations, not to mention all the interactions...”

Gurjun balsam, amyris, patchouli coeur, terpene and alpha-methylstyrene dimers, isolongifolanone, Trimofix ... next week we'll discuss the technological reproductions and ersatz versions, the depreciatory reductions and doctored perversions.

People chuckle at the association with reminiscences of 1960s fragrant counterculture, but the point of connection is usually missed. The organic expression served as a symbolic emissary from undefiled Creation, and its administration by hippies was a rebellious act.

Saffron sets out to explain, “Patchouli signified hope in the resurgence of Nature, and dabbing the oil was a way to affiliate with Earthly diversity, and to express that faith in the face of unlikelihood, to affirm the goodness of unspoiled Life, undeterred by its inherent disadvantage, being pitted against mainstream society, the biophobic dominating orthodoxy. So what if that's naive?"

Patchouli oil was never effective as an agent to mask cannabis smoke.

"Patchouli, the avatar of earth and roots, of the undomesticated, of leaves and spices, of the unadulterated, of the varying vital and whole, of the free fluxing and wild, of the uncorrupted."

Perfumes of History
(Rovesti)

This last class before our move to Mexico is a retrospective tour to identify junctures in the engineering of anti-Life machineries—the chemical makeover—let's have a look.

"Humanity has never been very pleased with how life goes, has never been accepting of how lives end. We offer the following tutorial chronicling the history of perfume in order to afford a good view of the ensuing drama," Saffron provides as introduction, adding, "the nature of olfactive perception is to land our focused attention at a salon to come," which is a separate question, that she's right to mention, as it bears on this topic.

The origin of perfumery with concentrated fragrant principles can be traced, thanks to Rovesti's discovery of an alembic-style distillation vessel, to the area covering part of present Pakistan roughly five thousand years ago, and blah blah ... how many times have you heard this flat recital? achh, tedious.

"Alembic from the Spanish *alambico* from the Arabic *al inbiq* from the Greek *ambix*, which means vessel."

Really, should we care precisely when or how or where the art and science of perfumery originated? whether it was the ancient

Chinese or early Egyptians cooking up oily odoraments? whether India's immemorial *chameli ka tel* (mmm, jasmine-soaked sesame oil) is traceable back two versus three thousand years?

"Perfume, the primary mode of contact among the living, the epitome of primal meaning in the matter of Life."

We've learned again and again, the term *perfume* derives from the Latin *perfumum* (through smoke) and ... well, listen—shall we agree here to dispense with the standard history lesson? and instead highlight events that have been surreptitiously spun by crafty conquistadores in chemistry? to suppress the actual material account that is the factual serial story of perfumery?

"Perfume, the original currency of vital connection, packed with nuanced indications and signals of urgent distress."

Perfume was never an ordinary vehicle, influencing courses of mystical and medical and other disparate lines of inquiry since antiquity. We're interested in the suspicious fate of this medium.

"Can you see the washers nuts and rivets teetering?"

Suspicious, why? Because volatile metabolites, storehouses of scentfully encoded information concerning Life, are vulnerable to subversive operations of extortion, of perfume piracy, hence our experience of sequestered chemical Nature has forever been co-opted by a line of surrogates and self-appointed mediators—priests alchemists shamans designers industrialists and ... predatory perfumers committed to remaking their prey into proxy perfumes, by reengineering the manifold aerial organic expressions of Life on Earth.

"Can you make out the cogs gears and bolts flying off the machine?"

Naturally, the ambitious program has courted a measure of blowback from Living Nature, but the schemers always double down with progressive ventures to decommission, to stow and scramble, as much as possible, the genuine communications of Creation.

"To be clear, this next instruction doesn't cover the full chronology of perfume on Earth, rather it's a story of sabotage carried out by our anteceding peers."

3000 B.C.—So our timeline must properly begin thousands of years before today if we are to abide Rovesti's terra cotta alembic discovery. But we've agreed to pass cursorily over subsequent dozens of centuries during which diverse cultures in areas now India and China, Pakistan and Egypt, appreciate aromatic compounds from Nature, which they use variously as found and augmented, to cure consecrate flavor barter and adorn.

"As resins, wines and ointments, incense, gums and unguents, plant juices, honeys and oleaginous seeds."

The earliest applications, which foreshadowed sophisticated solvent extraction techniques in waiting for several thousand years following, were based on a manner of physical diffusion common to procedures both primordial and continuing as we speak, in which odorful elements move from their source into watery (though aqueous tinctures are faint) and especially fatty or oily (much better) menstruums.

"The gist is in the matter of the mobile substances fashioned by Creation to be the most bioactive in the World."

But essential oil distillation is different, as the movement of metabolic messengers is primarily influenced by measure of volatility, along a divide of vapor pressure, not chemical compatibility. It appears that our ascendants of long ago had devised this exercise as an alternative to imbuing scents by soaking and impregnating. The method hinges on the capture of molecules relatively prone to vaporize, as they break away from a heated pot (retort) of plant matter (charge), on forcing their condensation and collection. (Though the implementation will become more efficient when water-cooled condensers are introduced ages later in eleventh-century Persia and employed in full swing by early sixteenth-century France.)

"And our interest in alchemy bears on the most ancient sensory faculty, you'll see."

750 (A.D. from this point on)—Our timeline jumps to here by skipping quite a few fragrant millennia of aromatica evolvement. Materials to register include: in the Orient, well-known products of jasmine and lotus and aloeswood, and a secretion for medicine from the musk deer ... in India, prominent scented wares of tuberose narcissus benzoin olibanum and of course sandalwood, animal products of civet and ambergris too ... in the Near East, celebrated anointing oils of spikenard myrrh saffron galbanum labdanum and cinnamon, the Arabian Peninsula a source of many.

"We are drawn to these elicitative fumes which we regard as cryptic confidences which we regard as evaporative voices of plants."

It appears that almost four thousand years pass during which there is little progress to improve methods of abducting the metabolic ciphers—can that be right? Apparently so. It's what we understand from historians of chemical technology, notwithstanding some scattered reports of Hellenistic advancements.

"We are keying on these enigmatic emanations which we regard as emissive etherealizations which we regard as storytelling vapors of Nature."

And Persian (Arab according to some) alchemist Abu Musa Jabir ibn Haiyan al-Azdl, shortened to Jabir ibn Hayyan, shortened further to the Latinized Geber for our benefit, designated the father of chemistry (paternity is of course disputed), is often credited with contributing a mighty upgrade to the sweeping enterprise of plant perfume appropriation: an alembic-type still with a retort tapered and curved to connect with another in such a way that aromatic volatiles, being liberated from heated plant material, on the escape, are condensed and isolated and purified. The innovative method is referred to as pure distillation and is destined to inspire alchemists of India and eventually medieval Europe.

"If we have time, we'd be remiss, not to recount in rhyme, if time permits, relative to the fortified wine, the work of Middle Ages alchemists, and their designs to press on, developing practices of distillation."

1025—The Persian scholar Avicenna (also Latinized, and don't call him an alchemist or his adherents will be affronted) is usually praised for laying the groundwork for modern methods of distillation, especially by steam. Here we're speaking about the various refined and embellished reflux vacuum and separatory techniques, and the liquefaction of vapors by means of the refrigerated coil.

"So straightaway, there is no longer the need to round up scent principles and squeeze them out from impregnated white wool."

Notice, in full swing now is the formidable project of flushing out, by virtue of their volatility, messaging metabolites from plants. Hang on to your hats—the grand program, rather benign so far, is soon to get ugly.

"We repeatedly hear that aroma oils queued for distillment are hardly to remain unscathed during their jarring entrainment by water vapor?"

To that we rejoin that it's true. With respect to this time-honored technology, certain volatile compounds that become subjected to a forced hot bath often react to produce artifacts such as chamazulene which newly appears in chamomile oil, or suffer hydrolysis such as that of esters, say, linalyl acetate which becomes diminished in proportion in lavender and clary sage essential oils. And a number of other molecular gains and losses and rearrangements are possible.

"The standard arguments presume an equivalency between distillates originating from growing and breathing beings and their industrial counterparts incorporating coal tar derivatives."

In any event, let's not get caught up on tripwires strewn by the everything-is-chemical clique. The familiar shtick of that bullying ilk serves their cynical sport prosecuted according to rules of zero-sum reduction. In Earth-based reality, we experience life in grades and extents, with little that's all-or-nothing. The straw-man parody holding the vitalist as a superstitious kook may go over well at Perfume Industry functions, but not here.

Yes, we affect plant volatiles in our capture, but how? to what degree? for what purpose? to whose benefit? detriment? risk? to yield what new to Nature? how much and how new? to what effects, be they evident or subliminal or even imperceptible?—all questions subsumed by a pressing concern before us: the fate met by infochemicals in the Natural World upon their seizure. Our attention isn't casual and we should do without condescension from the fraudful fraternity of neomanic fanatics in perfumery.

"The crusaders against Nature are anti-Life unto death, Earth-estranged with every breath, malevolently cavalier and disdainfully deaf to subtle and even blatant cries of Creation."

Perfumes of Meaning

"Non-Life is the rule, Life the troubling exception?"

Some radical perfumed pronouncements await our review, but we begin this evening with a query: why do birds fly southward when winter threatens?

"Because they would starve or freeze to death if they neglected to do so—because during their evolutionary trials they have acquired genes that impel them to make the trip—because they are triggered to take flight by hormonal changes ... which are in turn prompted by environmental stimuli ... such as decreasing hours of daylight—because a big storm or a sudden temperature drop sparks their migration ... which is guided by their perception of magnetic fields ... or by the sun that functions as a compass—because they follow other members of the flock ... as their parents taught them to do—because God created them to carry on this way."

Whether the answers are particular or general, meteorological or ontological, physiological or ecological, they're all believable, whether proximate or ultimate, they're all probably correct.

"To be straight, with regard to perfume, we aren't interested in how a given infochemical might make you feel, much as it is natural to take a hedonic inventory, still we don't encourage it."

And, whereas it is normal to consider the potential applications of an aromatic extract, still we're striving for something different ... we're prospecting for unnoted nuance, for subtle traces and novel contradictions, that might help us identify an elusive element like a cipher, perhaps embodied by some isomeric conformation, a chemical secret carried forth over epic evolutionary time, reflecting the back-and-forth pushing-and-pulling molecular discourse giving rise to creative assemblages of volatile metabolites in Nature, vital fragments of biological portfolios throughout the Natural World.

"We're seeking coded stories with lessons that reach us directly from the flowing fount of Creation."

... whoosh, pass the message—alpha-pinene plays a role in the communicative lives of zebra heliconian butterflies who drink from lantana flowers which incorporate—whoosh, pass the message—germacrene-d, which attracts American cockroaches who defend their physical integrity with a little help from—psst, pass the message—

"Still, I suspect, this deserves more consideration, the strategy of shaking down evocative vapors," Saffron says.

Short tales that deal with morality, called parables ... narratives that underpin cultures, called myths ... each speaks to the power of a great story, which is why we bother with these exercises, why we convene around storytelling perfumes preeminently prone to recount the dazzling saga of Creation.

"To present the story of perfume through history is to depict the pageant of Life on Earth."

... whoosh, pass the message—para-cresol, a koala messaging compound, blended into the marsupial's pheromonal urinary elixir along with—whoosh, pass the message—benzoic acid, employed by female African elephants to send molecular communiqués that comprise—psst, pass the message—

"The story has been cached and buried by a wayward civilization that would rather not pay attention."

...whoosh, pass the message—alpha-farnesene, which interweaves within the oleaceous headspace hanging over jasmine sambac plants in collaboration with—whoosh, pass the message—benzyl benzoate, an attractant used by foraging sweat bees in concert with—psst, pass the message—

Empyreal and material, poetic and empirical, we think it's a compelling story, and hope you'll agree, because the narrative is one of besiegement, and our aim here is to salute adherents and recruit proponents, those who will advocate on behalf of Living Creation.

...whoosh, pass the message—methyl salicylate, which submits to assist tuberose flowers to broadcast a diffusive message of abundance, luring face flies who place into courier service—whoosh, pass the message—skatole, a stercoraceous animal emission which also rises from blossoms of Indian jujube trees in coordination with other members of the chemical cocktail including—muah, pass the message—

Perfumes of Situation
(Angelica)

"The fragrant study before us relays tidings that show like a short little rondo in b-flat themed upon steamy forest floors, where snakes snuggle in soggy soil," Saffron opens up.

Do I have this right?—to coax away their scented souls, blossoms are ripped from plants by their pedicels, forcibly strewn on glass plates, glued down by sticky fat, left to die in their sleep ... then the disembodiment of spirit by the exodus of precious metabolic principles?

"It would be funny if it weren't a matter of life and death."

The faculty to communicate is an emergent yet characterizing attribute of Life, making its early appearance nearly four billion years ago with the first living entities and proliferating ever since, among biochemicals and cells and tissues, organs and organ systems and organisms, populations and communities and ecosystems, clearly as interactions across space, let alone the real case for communication along kinship lines through time.

"Upon first dipping of the root oil wafts a puff of pepper, then a rich verdant lifting voicing of herbal vapors timidly tempered by finicky folds of oozy wet smoldering wood," the panel begins to review extracts of angelica by first appreciating the volatile monoterpenes, namely the forwardly zestful phellandrenes.

Living beings communicate variously, but whether this is realized more or less manifestly or elusively or ubiquitously or understatedly or blatantly or faintly, whether by sounds for hearing or hues for seeing or animated displays for viewing . . . or by radiating perfumes for experiencing and perceiving by breathing, that is, by just being, communicative beings communicate. Even a dormant fungal spore is a message carried to the future, and any organism alive is similarly a missive to generations following with specifications concerning how to live.

"The Slovakian oil is oily and the smoke is that of dry tobacco—we recognize our next sample dilution, which vaguely implies cumin, by its oblique swampish tones and the earthy allusion to pitchy juniper, and for its dispersive diffusion of heady animal-fatty notes," also circulating are samples of distillates from India and France and Hungary.

And, as Life on Earth is an elaborate long-running epical story comprising circumstantial particularities, with each development embedded in some setting and contingent upon what came before, biological information is inseparable from its context.

"Even DNA doesn't hold a key to its own interpretation."

The oil from seeds, which I'd call seedy, "puts out a pungent pronouncement, pervasively acrid and exuberantly spicy—with sheer facets of anise that seem to vanish—it's a scentful representation like a layered construction, of rotting oranges moldering on mowed grass—or an old shoe stained with resiny glue which is holding together the mildewed leather."

So, inasmuch as chemical couriers make up the primary and prevailing currency of information among the living, the fundamental language of Life on this planet, then these organic odoraments stand to lose contextual meaning when wrested from their sources and surroundings.

"A toned-down animal element swells after some minutes to give off an indication that's vaguely caramelic and plainly erogenic—next, accents and flourishes of coffee and heliotrope and coumarin and compost imbue the fringes of spaces like tinges and traces of top-notes and bases." The suggestion of erogeneity is likely a reference to the lactone cyclopentadecanolide, a genuine Nature-made rendering of the more widely encountered synthetic musk Exaltolide marketed by the Swiss concern Firmenich to the crass human movement of mass imprudent perfumery.

So, insofar as an aromatic oil is displaced, in theory a densely compressed wellspring of vital ciphers but now sealed up and isolated in a hermetic glass enclosure and far removed from its provenance, we lose situational information?

Any ideas?

"Seeing that the elegant architecture of chemical Creation hinges on context, then instead of fixing on fixed snapshots marked by our fingerprints, we might rather carry on otherwise, to showcase the molecular hodgepodge as Nature guides ... instead of studying disembedded slices we might rather tour the unprocessed and unabducted, the altogether undisrupted natural habitats of expressive Life?"

Any other ideas?

Perfumes of Prospect

"Now, to set the meeting in motion, our first salon this side of the Tropic of Cancer, or more accurately, our first blending workshop—*saludos bienvenidos* and all that," Saffron leads into our ritual.

Shall we each introduce ourselves? nah, no matter, let's get going—to compose organic perfumes by the method of combining infochemical effusions *de la naturaleza*, as promised, to assemble a fragrant accord in accord with its own fragrant tendencies. You'll receive no handouts, so we suggest you chronicle the exercise.

"...lest the content become cached to some *rincón inaccesible de la mente*, by which we refer to no remote mental cranny in particular."

The gist is to discover how volatile plant extracts from seeds herbs and fruits, flowers woods and roots, may be blended to favor the emergence of a singular aesthetic expression, a new molecular medley of compressed information.

"A chemical collaboration of immeasurable elaboration."

Some of you have been enticed by the dimensional allure of perfumery? the provocative nature of the evocative vapors? the sexy suggestiveness, alchemical interplay, shrouded mystique, overt rejection of sterile logic? the call to create vibrant living compositions? to download the intangible? the prospect of opportunity to better understand our natural heritage by means of transformational art?

"Of the ideal and the real, this is the real deal."

I've been told that my expositions are a bit stretched out (am I running on still? earning my reputation?), but these sessions and studies aren't about me, you'll see. The contemplation we do is outwardly directed, in that all our self-centered mindsets will yield to our scented subjects, and all our self-awareness will shift and attune to perceive previously eluding vapory principles that travel across spaces and bear resonant indications.

"Goodbye unifying centripetal forces, hello atomizing centrifugal effects."

But first, this excursive warning, to immunize against some infectious ideas: there will be no diplomas or certificates awarded, no plaques or titles, no curriculum credits, no guides or directives to facilitate careers in perfumery, no lectures on functional applications or value chains or financial audits or balance sheets or performance indices or packaging or market research or commercial evaluation or quality control, no candles or creams, soaps or medicines, no take-home party favors at all, clear enough?

"So what products do you sell, Dr. Von Hohenheim, errr, Bombastus, errr, Theophrastus?" Names for Paracelsus?

I won't bother recounting all my clumsy bids to field the tedium of such inquiries, but in order to leave and not return to this subject, I've stitched together and finally settled on a countering condensation, something like my *aleluya* mantra at the ready: Money Ruins Everything.

"All set for searching?"

Remember, William Blake would burn his poetry, didn't intend to sell it, didn't even want anyone to read it, complained of being devoured by jackals, or were they hyenas? And Van Gogh too, he painted pictures to demonstrate the beauty of certain plants and landscapes, corresponded with brother Theo in the matter of sales because he needed to purchase food and supplies.

"Ready for action?"

You may wish to wear loose comfortable clothing ja-ja, as momentarily we'll set out after unfettered truth and beauty. We'll welcome the creative impulse, but don't bother with the facade of art, or be concerned about any veil of mind. You'll see, you'll gather, why the perfumed testimony of Nature is the medium of choice for relating messages that matter.

"Psyched-up for delving?"

You'll soon learn how it is that bundled formations of metabolic improvisation avail as an impactful antidote to the trouble with art.

"Primed for engagement?"

To complete my thought—artists wrestle to reconcile substance and idea, and strive to make their preferred stock media come to life. Rumi wished his words wouldn't appear as words. Pollack regarded pigments similarly. And Coltrane grappled with the tones of his soprano sax. How would they all do to fashion artworks with an organic medium that reverberates with everything alive?

"The most perfect picture, nothing more than a warty threadbare approximation, a dry porridge—so does a founding Dadaist express inadequacy of art by instruments and vehicles on hand, helpless to ignite a full-on unmediated adventure of instinct sense."

Artists are unwittingly deprived of access to the transmissible principles that constitute the primary mode of communication on Earth, the rich emissive palette developed over thousands of thousands of millennia, of materializations that are truly high-fidelity expressions of Nature, being the vital currency of creation, by which we mean Creation, concerning which we mean perfume.

"So, everyone, find vial numbered one, and listen carefully..."

Perfumes of Apprisal

(A prospective salon—may I promote this?—it features wormwood and the intrigues of absinthe—coming soon.)

"Question: where on a woman's body should she apply a commercial perfume? Answer: wherever she doesn't want to be kissed," Saffron initiates the proceeding.

Alcoholic libations are celebrations of interplay between life and death, incorporating, on the one hand, volatile compounds that form the major messaging system of living beings and, on the other, ferment product alcohol to provide the underpinning theme of decay.

(Saffron again calls on guests to be seated by tap-tapping her spoon *clink-clink* to the side of an absinthe glass.)

Recall those beginning biology class drills on basic bioenergetics? about anabolism and catabolism, biosynthetic pathways yielding carbohydrate energy stores and the complementary metabolic reactions to make calories available?

"To be sure, the class material seemed tedious at the time."

Really, the subject is heavier than weighty, the topic beyond far-reaching, being the study of Life, of profound science and pure poetry, of growth and decomposition, accumulation and disintegration, blending and dissolution, flourishing and decline.

"Rectification and purification, cohobation and fraction-ation … to sever then splice, move apart then bring together, break up then make up and marry, all that?"

Sugar in the presence of oxygen is sometimes persuaded to provide living organisms with a metabolic helping hand (energy), and by doing so will split up into carbon dioxide and water. Or instead, the pathway of fermentation may be followed, to turn out perhaps lactic acid or ethanol (resting on the presence of oxygen and certain bacteria or yeast organisms) as is common throughout Nature.

"All this is to announce the upcoming plant perfume soirée, to celebrate *la fée verte*, that is to say … absinthe."

In woodlands and deserts and grasslands and marshes, alco-hols and other diverse breakdown products of organic mate-rial routinely combine in immeasurably elaborate ways with vaporous information-rich molecules of Life to compose cock-tails of creation and decay. Our controlled extractions selec-tively intercept these Janus-themed chemical alliances, and by our operations we aspire to reveal and celebrate the Nat-ural World by pointing up exalting expressions of biocultural variation.

"In the absinthe drink, within the solution, there is a bitter-sweet interplay of wormwood principles with anisic elements."

Absinthe has by culture and chemistry earned a good spot of notoriety, but the aperture of our attention will center on the inimitable production process. Your salon host (yours truly) will lead a discussion concerning the art and science of capturing and blending molecules from Living Nature, elegantly exempli-fied by the distilled spirit of our interest. Cocktails and aromatic extracts will be distributed and reviewed.

"You kindle my curiosity in Janus the Roman door god who faces indoors and out."

If you haven't yet served on a perfume panel, the premise of the observance rests on our recognition of scentful metabolites as the primary wellspring of information in the matter of the enigmatic phenomenon of Life on Earth. So we tap assorted volatile fragments of biological portfolios in order to gain insights into the nature of Nature. Samples of extracts, by means of imbuing special strips of blotter paper called *touches à sentir*, are passed around for partakers to behold. Impressions are shared and we endeavor to ignite lines of inquiry.

"The curious craft of molecular mixology will be specifically revealed in fragrant detail."

Our aim is to line up an ensemble of cognoscenti, aficionados and connoisseurs with a variety of life histories and proclivities, aromancers and artists, gastronomes and philosophers of beauty, freaks and fanatics, geeks and oenologists, *non-conformistes* and naturalists, as well as savants in modern perfumery.

"Whereas the latter faction are known to display cleverness of means, they'll also be challenged to demonstrate the wisdom of their intentions."

Perfumes of Sequestration
(Immortelle)

"Welcome to our celebration of vitalism in which we invite detailed description of particular perfumes from practical plants living humdrum lives in a material World," Saffron starts up.

Ready? for olfactive exploration? of Nature's vapors? that is, a selection of powerhouse elicitations distilled from populations of helichrysum, that is, from the oil we call everlast or everlasting or immortelle, which is our metabolic friend and ally, with which we deeply affiliate.

"The plants also go by the name *petit soleil d'or* or sometimes by *sempreviva*, to signify that they appear never to wither during drought or hot weather."

Panel members begin contributing in turns, "This sample connotes a hovering headspace over an herbal tisane of liquorice and chamomile and ginger—it displays something like shades summoning a summer in Europe and sugary syrup that caramelizes under the Mediterranean sun—and broadcasts not only the stock floaty first-blush phenolic lift which plays up the first-flush fine-tea-like facet but also concurrently a first-kiss-like expression that gives the impression of lemon."

Chemical profiles notably high in neryl acetate characterize volatile oils from Corsica, collectively distinguishable from those high in alpha-pinene from the Balkans. Taxonomists separate these chemotypes at the subspecific level (though the oil we commonly designate as helichrysum oil gymnosephalum is from an altogether distinct species).

The visiting salonists carry on like sensory sleuths, "A component of this oil is curcumin, which is a famous feature in turmeric, which is a masala staple, which explains the fragrant factor that's remindful of the balmy ambience inside an Indian grocery store?—the herb is referred to as curry plant (the etymology is not culinary but organoleptic)—there's a layered construction of back-and-foreground features such as the whiffy flourishes of pickled fruity relishes—I may be deliriously sensing reflections of wormwood and ham?—mimosa and butter and sage?—the unique aromatic identity owes to a chemistry which effects a mowed-grassy constancy and a minimal impartment of coumarinic compounds which we liken to slight sounds in a dense symphony."

"Coumarin calls to mind the scent of ... coumarin. (We have a problem, we know.)"

In theory, you can depict a perfume epithetically, by denoting a given quality, as you would a hue or musical pitch.

"Fenchone conveys the scentful idea of ... fenchone. (We have a lexical issue. It's complicated.)"

Let's first put aside the thwarting notion that each olfactive sensation is itself a composite effect, of a conglomerative compound summed of individual atomic bonds emitting electromagnetic vibrations at specific wave numbers in the infrared range.

"Benzyl acetate typifies the scent of ... benzyl acetate. (We have a terminological predicament.)"

So then, let's resolve that the aroma sent forth by a given molecule can be referenced using the name of that same molecule. And indicated also by the denominal adjective: linalol strikes us as linalolic, borneol as borneolic, 1,8-cineole as cineolic, camphor as camphorous—

"Camphoraceous."

But essential oils from savory sandalwood and saffron, from basil bay and bergamot don't merely dispatch simple collections of odor traces, rather they are higher-order composite perfumes, aggregations of molecular chords, combinations of combinations, reflecting new levels of organization, new dimensions and extents of biological exponentiation. The increased complexity frustrates our naming them straightly and artlessly.

"A fragrant missive is lavandaceous owing to an association with the estery perennial herb, yet the label *lavender* denotes the source of the fragrance, not the fragrance itself."

The thrust of this discourse can be summarized by pointing out that aromatic expressions on Earth are countless, that perfumes of Nature vary from point to point in space and from moment to moment in time, while new synthetic odorants are ever multiplying. The practice of associative depiction can sometimes help us to supply identifying information, but eventually fails our efforts. And we're also deprived of any correlative nomenclature for the direct and objective characterization of perfume.

"*Ludibrium materiae*, the subtle hoax of matter."

Color may be bright saturated vivid light dark ... music may be fast slow percussive loud quiet ... haptic feeling may reveal substances to be coarse smooth hot cold ... the terminology is straightforward if not unambiguous. Scent also may be loud coarse vivid dark sparkly pungent cool and so on, these terms serving as synesthetic metaphor, their signification often indistinct or obscure depending on the synesthesia-sense of the author, along with that of the audience.

"This next comes across as a spongy serving of a marmalady compote of plummy prunes—with a melting helping of nut butter and honey-soaked straw or caramel-saturated hay—coated by gummy maple sugar—underpinned by rich balsamic amber— boosted by green salted curry sauce? exalted by toasty smoky apioid spices?—altogether eliciting a leafy wood-planky gin-dry blend of fenugreek and tobacco and orange pekoe—it releases an etherealization as if it unleashes a discharge of dissipating shots of turkish coffee or toffee like a tonka-flavored transitory back-story."

So, to describe plant perfumes we have the exercise of name identification or association with botanical sources or volatile compounds, we have hedonic reactions, we have our reminiscences, and those disposed toward figurative representation have a vast menu of metaphor options, but we have a lousy barren dictionary for specific concrete unmitigated description.

"This Corsican rendering comes on dusty though the mustiness is repressed, it's especially rich and more floral than the rest—seems creamy in an oily way—or oily in a seedy way— more seedy in a celery-seed or dill-weed way—secretes a scattering of accents as well, like wisps of waxes and resins and hints of butterscotch and turpentine—a puff of powder is intimated just barely—in any respect, the principal thematic evocation is of burnt sucrose."

The *aromathérapie* community in the West, a wee syco-phantic sorry to suggest, heeds the preferences of pioneer and helichrysum-champion Kurt Schnaubelt, who exclusively favors oils of Corsica Island provenance, where plants grow in abun-dance among maquis and garigue vegetation of myrtle and cistus and rosemary.

"This absolute is from Bosnia-Herzegovina, the sticky brew of metabolites being thicker and darker and harder to work with, more deeply hued and heavily coumarinic in compari-son to distillates, a kind of wafting interplay of elements, the vegetal most prevalent, and the animal, yes present but less evident."

To supplement our own survey we read reports about a pop-ulation of helichrysum *gymnocephalum* that turns out brisk blowy notes that verge on being minty but are more accurately termed cineolic, and a conspecific taxon that lets off apricot and pine-needle principles succeeded by a drydown recalling soapy guaiacwood, and a different transmission with a lavandaceous structure that is issued by helichrysum *bracteatum* plants, and another extract derived from helichrysum *stoechas* inflores-cences that makes an exhibit of metabolic references to raisins dung and leather.

The subject of discussion now shifts:

"We require a key, a rosetta stone to gain information from our captive compounds, to productively interrogate our chemi-cal abductees."

With Life on the edge, our pressing challenge is that of deci-pherment, to interpret the fundamental messaging medium of Nature, that is, the primary means of organic expression, that is, the essential language of plants.

"The question is worth raising of how we're to unscramble ordering principles, tap into the wellspring, unwrap layers of evolutionary encryption, translate the vocabulary of Nature, which has become unduly exotic."

In the matter of our presumption of linguistic unity throughout Creation, of some common proprietary chemical lexicon shared among all the World's flora, I have my doubts, I don't need to say.

"Audible communication between cicadas is different from that between finches, which is a dialect different from that employed by prairie dogs?"

A molecular code perhaps, in the form of individualized ciphers of distinct designation that correspond to particularities in the service of all biological Life.

"No matter, there is work cut out for us."

Perfumes of Presage
(Grasse)

1190—Continuing our survey through time, water-cooled distillation condensers are now in common use, and crusaders have been returning to Europe from faraway conquests, bearing all sorts of aromatic treats. And alcohol, long since discovered, is gaining momentum to impress with its wondrous amphiphilic properties for perfumery.

But let's take a moment to take notice of something that's becoming more noticeable, of hiddenness that is becoming less hidden, of clandestinity becoming harder to ignore and secretiveness becoming more evident.

"The odorful principles of plants have long been regarded as curiously incomparable, their sequestering with heated water reveals a kind of substance uniquely unique," Saffron just now arrives.

Surprised? that relative to other historic aspects of cultures, again and again is a paucity of records? that precious few recipes were written down, or sacramental rites detailed? that concealed compositions are lock-and-key guarded, be they formulae of medieval alchemists or apothecary pharmacists or ancient

Egyptian priests? This dearth goes a ways to explain why historians have been so challenged to describe aromatic culture of antiquity.

"Chemical communications ... they're mythic, if not sanctified ... cryptic, if not classified."

Around this time, the aura of exclusivity and elevated status for perfumery are encouraged in France as master perfumers are granted a charter by King Philip Augustus, a required course of training is stipulated, and the bar of entry raised. This sort of official recognition would not be the last, as various institutions of power will continue to promote the visage of elitism.

"All this bodes the nature of mass perfumery to come."

1420—The cooling-with-cold-water condenser is upgraded again, this time by its reshaping into an elongated coil to improve the efficiency of intercepting infochemical compounds.

1500—The essential oil trade comes into its own now as distillation is more widely carried out. Granted, elements in Nature are confronted more aggressively, yet emissive fragrances are still encumbered in a way that minimizes trauma (mostly), as volatile oils survive the ordeal relatively intact (usually), the chemical heist mimicking natural processes (to a degree), by which we refer to the sequestration of nutrients, the transformation of metabolites, cycles of evaporation and condensation, to the moving and morphing of molecules in wind and water and on furs and seeds and—

"Furs seeds and insect proboscises."

And not coincidentally, the art of perfumery forges ahead, still to most shrouded and out of reach, still customarily associated with medicine or nobility or the occult, but progressively with a palette for perfumers broadened to include not only tinctures and waters and oily macerates but also the more concentrated distillates of fragrant plants.

"Around this time in southern France, humanity professes its love for vaporous expressions of Nature with a historic burst of innovative demonstration."

Yes, we acknowledge with some sentimentality that the Grasse perfume industry is more or less fully fledged by now. They seem there to be faithfully improving their methods, guilelessly refining their reverent practices of gentle seduction and respectful coaxing, their well-intended operations to summon and foster the scentful secretions of plants.

"The developments call to my mind a romantic relationship that appears outwardly to be flourishing but is actually in trouble, perhaps done for."

As we'll see, groundwork is laid in Grasse for rougher treatments upcoming and the eventual flat-out undermining and violation by humankind of sensuous Nature.

(Class breaks.)

"But before we move on, let's pause for just a flash, to tip our hats and recognize the eminent alchemist of these times who conceived of the term *essential oil*, the Swiss medical man Paracelsus, who set about interpreting the novel aromatic substance obtainable from plants by entrainment with steam, which he judged to be an expression of Nature fortified beyond its grade, the soul or innermost nature of the plant, so incomparable as to be designated, alongside earth water fire and air, the fifth classical element—the element of imbued Life—the *quinta essentia* or quintessence, essence being the spirit of the thing. So upon extraction, we have in the oil the drawn-out spirit of the thing—the essence oil—the essential oil."

Perfumes of Departure

"The wealthy are never assigned the task of cleaning up all the running blood."

Our aromatic holdings include expressions of random interest, some being rare captive compounds we're to consult with, keeping in mind that these fragrant hearings are not just for pleasure. Saffron has labored to prepare samples:

"Tagete oil is from marigold, not French but a different species, not calendula but a different genus, this one distilled from wild-gathered naturalized (khaki bush) plants in South Africa—the leading toppy effluvial elements are oppressively heady and aggressively green, being persistently between intensely fruity and acutely winey like the morning after a bacchanalia at a winery—worse, the bracing vapors are penetrating and migraine-summoning—the full ambience owes to a headspace that embraces traces considerable as herbaceous and saponaceous and rutaceous and graminaceous (good gracious)—also ceding to our review is an Indian sample with a verdant sulfury exterior, an Egyptian more grape-juicy with a delayed ketonic transmission, and a Malagasy that is near-citrusy and becomes slightly cellulosic."

The harvesting and reengineering of Nature pumps up

currencies and resources to heat up local economies causing upheaval of vulnerable long-established traditions and ecologies of place, decimating wild lands and the public realm, never benefiting the ancestral nor the time-honored, always to the detriment of the voiceless and dispossessed.

"An integrally congruous herby camphorous curvy facade levels out with a gentle gigantic berrylike heart becoming very jammy like plummy cherry jelly—(yes, I'm partial to this) Hungarian yarrow (milfoil, sneezewort) distillate—this volatile oil is quarry-deep cobalt blue owing to molecules of chamazulene— the early thujonish flourishes are suggestive of cedarleaf but here tinged additionally with a vegetable character, and also a generous cineolic twist, the aggregate emissive ensemble maturing as soft impressions of carrot seed and tobacco, finally giving off a faint indication of desiccated cardboard—another version to behold is a cerulean emissary from England, less alimentary but more medical-zesty, then lastly straw-grassy."

Who will speak on behalf of sticking with what has worked? with what has sufficed? for age-old systems that have provided a mixed bag of rewards and hardships? Now, as communities of animals and plants and people are busted apart, often violently, Nature's services and social supportive structures are dismantled (you old-timers with temporary factory work will surely be devastated when the merciless industrialists are done with you).

"It's not deer musk no, though musky nonetheless yes, not from an animal's rectal area no, though evocative nonetheless yes, it's a little nutty a little soapy a little creamy a little grape-pulpy, and yes it's very (vegetally) musky, but then it must be musky being designated *musk mallow?*—ambrette seed absolute, derived from a tropical hibiscus confamiliar, is more accurately depicted as a waxy solid essential oil (ambrette *beurre*) that's been fractionated to yield an oily oil from seedy seeds—our tincture in alcohol is vinous and flowery and seems to exhale dust?—and this next is an ambrette attar (who knew?) that at once elicits our olfactive inferences of senses of sweetness and fattiness and references to dryness and waxiness—and from this last sample, a stale clary-like oil, we find flashing an ethereal principle, perhaps ambrettolide, by which we refer to the plant metabolite, not its ubiquitous synthetic replacement."

Data, charts, facts and figures, never reveal the drudging nature of new jobs created—

"...nor the heartsickness of those who've migrated from modest countryside dwellings (wasn't much but it was home) to some desolate slum where the experience of human dignity is not practicably sustainable."

And locales that exhibit a sense of place still, where idiosyncratic charm hasn't yet been stamped out, where farmers and artisans and poets might reside, even seekers like some of us here, who try to eek out lives with looser connections to Nature-ravaging machineries of accumulation ... such scattered livable pockets eventually become appealing also to the ambassadors of amassment, so these places for them become courts or sinks for dumping their dirty money.

"*Adios*, bye-bye."

Perfumes of Purpose

(I'm thinking about the original pitch I made to interest Saffron.)

Prospective apprentices took their seats and I at once began an improvised orientation (initiation, whatever it was, I should have been better prepared), emphasizing various disciplines of inquiry:

Briefly (oh sure), so that you'll realize what you're in for if you join with this enterprise—you'll need to revisit, brush up, and accomplish command, of laboratory tools and techniques, strategies and methods, of medicinal perfumery and magico-sacramental applications, chemical ecology and biological semiotics, structural formulae shorthand and mass-spec gas-chromatographic analyses, lots more.

I sensed my audience fading.

We produce no products, only one-of-a-kind expressions of personal efforts to come to terms with the World, of art, poetry, and prayer, as we preside over alchemical transformations of fancy into form and back again, embrace the metaphysics of blending, investigate both gifts of Nature and entrails of Industry, trace biosynthetic pathways of Creation, emphasize the realm of botanical perfumes in which metabolic vapors implore an audience—we go deep, we penetrate, it's serious business (and remember, don't touch my Rancilio espresso machine).

The company, eventually to disperse—as if I were kidnapper and they my hostages?—provided a familiar collection of excuses, some polite questions, guestbook entries, but no commitments.

(I find myself recounting a first acquaintance.)

Now there is quiet. Sitting in my makeshift studio, which is littered with fading scent strips, with vials and pipettes, alcohol and dropper bottles, I'm alone except for a single person. After the others have left, she's remained (I suppose that carries some currency)? She helps clean the mess (virtually all of it, I admit).

Saffron (nice name) barely introduces herself but matter-of-factly declares that she'll be back to begin work tomorrow, though I never invited her apprenticeship? I don't make out anything exceptional about her (don't pay much attention) except to notice that she's finishing my sentences for me (handily).

The day following she returns, thanks me for the opportunity, says that she's a fearless and serious eager seeker and is taken with my idea that profound instruction is revealed by deeply seated secret ciphers of Nature. She says that she's pleased I scared away all other candidates for the position, that I appeared as an overbearing blustery nut-case (I did give an uncertain impression, I admit).

I ask, How's your Spanish?

"Enough for my purposes."

Because I'll soon be setting southward, relocating, to further the campaign, in a high-elevation sierra where reduced atmospheric pressure invites all various perfumes to spring from their origins, volatile molecules determined not to be ignored, or misunderstood, or skirted, not in highland Central Mexico, where I'm heading.

"*La mierda tiene consecuencias.*" I've no idea what she means by this, if anything.

Perfumes of Affiliation
(Espresso)

❧

"For this master class, your Salonnier has adapted highlights of an original review that he presents to molecular baristas," Saffron makes the opening remarks.

We begin near the beginning (indulge me), with the first organic interfaces, membranes separating the *caldo* of chemicals interior from those exterior to an organism, giving rise to the earliest expressions of individual identity, eventually begetting—after a few billion years of testing, of trial-and-error propagating and generating—natural diversity, the splendorous variety of Creation.

"The heterogeneous family of coffee kin, the rubiaceous troop of taxa we assign to the Rubiaceae, are uncommonly celebrated for their contributions to human civilization."

Central to understanding the agency of perfume in the World is this fundamental structural interface, the biological mother of all biological interfaces, the primary interface of Life. This semi-permeable selective bilayer phospholipid membrane, formed of a vital non-watery lipophilic stratum bounded on each side with a hydrophilic layer, is notably discriminating of water-friendly (polar) substances seeking to cross the barrier, whereas it is more welcoming (passage is more readily granted) to oil-friendly molecules. Oleo-affinitive compounds (perfumes!) are therefore by chemical design more biologically active, and in consequence are favored carriers of information among living beings.

"The botanical family of rubes includes ... quinine and gardenia, woodruff and karo-karounde ... and coffee, the most consumed (apart from water) beverage on the planet."

These molecular messengers (perfumes!), these volatile couriers (perfumes!) mostly prefer to associate with lipidic rather than aqueous substances, affiliate more with oil-inviting rather than water-inviting tissues, including the physiological membrane-based mechanisms of chemical perception (to behold perfumes!) employed by organisms of diverse derivation throughout the kingdoms of Life.

"Yeasty bread and rice steam, pencil shavings and burnt peanuts, freshly peeled apples and soppy sugarcoated cereal," Saffron recounts depictions drawn during our latest convivial cupping exercise.

It is on account of this characteristic physiochemical behavior that an accomplished chef would never attempt to prepare a hearty soup using a stock of plain unembellished water. Broths contain oily or fatty compounds summoning to liposoluble flavors from ingredients like herbs and spices. And adding to this effect are amphipathic compounds with affinities to both polar and non-polar molecules, say in creamy *sopas* for example, where the casein protein in milk fulfills this function.

"Sauvignon grape and lemon zest, pipe tobacco and hot compost, rotten bananas and warm gingerbread, garden peas and redcurrant jelly, tanned leather and ambrosial jasmine."

And the implications in this matter are illustrated with the help of my Rancilio Silvia *cafetera* ... which provides on good days nine times sea-level atmospheric pressure to force hot water through a compacted bed of finely ground roasted coffee endosperm to yield an intricately involved full-bodied concentrated richly aromatic bittersweet brew topped with a culminating layer of *crema* that imparts a pleasantly lingering aftertaste!

"So affirms our salon leader as he pulls his fifth shot of espresso in the course of the last hour."

Among chemicals within the green unprocessed seeds is a conglomerative substance of densely stored energy. The mixture is primarily lipidic though it also consists of many oxygenated polar compounds. Designated *coffee essence* or *coffeöl*, it is key to our inquiry, as nearly a thousand emissive principles have been recognized (more identifications to come) in the headspace of this material upon its expression from cherries, so-named coffee fruits.

"I don't grasp why in the Natural World so many fragrant metabolites would be cloistered beneath thick layers of pericarp tissue? never to be perceived by monkeys or elephants or other agents of dispersal?"

We wonder about all the various components of this coffee oil. We are particularly curious about where the vaporous bounty goes upon preparation of the drink. This central question is up for debate, and the answer will mark out the idea of this entire discourse.

"Nor do I fathom how the majority of odorants in the beans survive processing by people?"

The hot roasting drums especially cause quite a chemical stir, as sugars are caramelized and complex carbohydrates degraded and enzymes denatured. So, cooking the faster the better is least

destructive, yet still, carbs and proteins are substantially trans-
formed by the roasting. In any event, during this operation, the
lipids break down much less relative to other constituents—
that's a hint—a tip-off on the question posited, concerning the
riddling fate of all those perfume principles.

"Along with the molecular undoing from heating comes also
the generation of new flavor compounds such as pyrazines (nou-
gat roasted toasted cereal) and pyrroles (mellowed molasses
maple mushrooms)."

Take this as a clue, or as a review, as in a reiteration, or a
preview for some of you? of the foundation of our explanation:
that oily oils travel well together with essential oils, the latter
bestowed by Creation with the capacity for easy sequestration,
then storage then mobilization then dispatch by plants for messaging, then the demonstration of exceptional transmissibility
and then the culmination, the property of permeability across
olfactive tissues of percipients.

"And then ... smoky 2-methoxy-4-vinylphenol and then ...
fresh-roasty 3-methyl-2-butene-1-thiol and then ... burnt-roasty
furfuryl mercaptan and then ... mocha-roasty furfuryl methyl
disulphide?"

All right, let's try a different approach to work this out:

Practices for drawing out or intercepting molecular communications from beings in Nature lend themselves to organizing into three categories—one cluster defined by properties of
chemistry, the next established by effects that are physical, the
last bound together by forces that are mechanical.

The first grouping encompasses extractions delineated
primarily on the basis of dissolubility, chemical interactions
between volatile metabolites and a chosen menstruum, a

dissolving medium. These operations comprise, for instance, alcohol maceration to yield a tincture (say, vanilla extract) and water steeping to give an infusion or decoction (like tea) and solvent extraction to provide a resinoid (such as benzoin) or a nineteenth-century *extrait* (pronounced extray) or a *pommade* or *absolue d'enfleurage* (we have a sample of tuberose) or a modern *concrète* or absolute (like orange flower).

The second circumscription follows a different strategy, whereby techniques to capture and separate and concentrate principles of scent adhere to a different set of physical laws. The elemental method is governed by vapor pressure, by volatility— termed *distillation*, it is often carried out with water or steam or both, in stills of glass or copper, steel or clay, primitively over wood fires or sophisticatedly under vacuum, to yield distillates including (liquors of course, and) the vast range of essential oils produced.

And the third class of appropriated aromatic emissions results from processes that are forceful, accomplished by exerting pressure, by squeezing or pressing plant tissues saturated with oils. The familiar case is that of citrus fruit rinds wherein the volatiles are extruded from the outer hesperidium walls. In this way, the target essential oils bypass the solvents or steam of corresponding treatments, and so better retain their oxygenated components.

So now, the crux of the challenge is to make out where within the classification are different coffee preparations to be assigned.

"First, our doorkeeper our balm our true secret vessel."

Java beverages made with percolators or drip-through filters are extractions that depend upon measures of solubility, of the coffee constituents in Nature's major constant solvent, the elegant preeminent solvent of the Natural World, the solvent with the involvement with everything alive.

"In rain puddles and hot tubs, as seltzer and snow, this solvent is the one to which we owe the morning cup-of-joe."

A common cup of coffee, the aqueous solution of sugars and acids, protein-like materials and lots of hydrophilic caffeine, among other mostly polar compounds, is sponsored by water.

"Just by the description, I begin to feel flushed and sweaty, dehydrated and edgy."

Caffeine is concentrated along leaf margins of coffee plants where herbivorous insects often first set about their assault. The alkaloid also collects in pollen grains of flower stamens, thereby passing along to pollinating bees, who subsequently exhibit broad enhanced activity, stimulated to better defend their hives against hornets.

"The busy bees become even busier."

So now, you'll notice the drift as we arrive at the gist of this lesson ... that espresso stands apart from most other coffee drinks.

"I detect some of those distinguishing scentful vapors ... the wafting winey and earthy ambience ... the bitter balmy and buttery tones of bakers chocolate and brown sugar—"

In the matter of the mechanism of production, espresso is comparable to freshly squeezed juices and cold-pressed olive oils, the compression of comminuted endosperm cake being the decisive distinction, the forceful coercion of minute lipoids that are mostly unresponsive to the coaxing of hot-water extractive washing.

"... a creamy impression of tree balsams ... a pulpy sensation of dried fruit ... a doughy suggestion of hazelnuts ... a sulphury presence of cooked beef ... a nectareous reference to caramelized pineapple—"

Derivation of the word *espresso* is from the Latin *esprimere*, meaning to press out, which we accomplish with machines engineered for this purpose, to effect a pressurized sequestration of oil globules that would otherwise stay put.

"Next thing, we're going on about rubbery robustas and syrupy arabicas, dry-grassy monsooned Indian specialties and plump sun-kissed apricot-jellyish Ethiopian imports."

So now, we've arrived finally to address the sum and substance of this study, the fortunes of the principal principles of our interest, the free ride afforded those certain select compounds, the commute of those vapory hitchhikers along with tiny expressed oil droplets.

"It should be plain to recognize, perfume!"

They are lipid-loving multiplex molecules of mother-tongue messaging, in the service of the currency of communication compelled by Creation. They are fragrant notices and instructions composed in the first-chosen language, the original primordial and prevailing medium for the passage of information relating to Life.

"It's not a far cry in its drinking guise, perfume!"

We recommend to drink the oil-in-water emulsion soon after it drips into pre-warmed cups, whereas adding some milk will extend that best-by window of time for maximal appreciation.

"Flavors (perfume!) will linger in the pharynx for a few minutes, since those perfume-pulling lipids are attracted to mouth membranes and so invite and lengthen the retention of the suspension on the tongue."

First you inhale: in the headspace hovering above the demitasse is an aromatic spectrum of lipophilic volatiles (perfume!) that find their way to your perception by the orthonasal route (through the nares). Then you have a sip: dissolved in the dispersed lipidic phase of the brew are more of those fragrant metabolites in tow (perfume!)—after reacting in complex ways with the biotic environment of your mouth, they travel as gaseous molecules reaching your olfactive tissues by the retronasal, the pharyngeal route (originating in the oral cavity).

"More sought, more found ... driving away and coming around ... are indications of cucumber oysters and anise and toffee and coriander cocoa and barley and curry and pralines and chestnut and cardamom caraway nutmeg and custard and incense and cedarwood."

Then there's the *crema* ... much as this top layer is an unstable chemical emulsion (technically a colloid) facilitated by local amphiphiles, the emulsive effect is compounded by its foaminess, thus it functions additionally as a gas-in-liquid emulsion. The bubbly effervescent interface acts as both a protective layer and amplifier, modulating the release of aroma principles (perfume!) that are weakly entrapped while at the same time provided with increased surface area to launch.

"The volatiles (perfume!) are both preserved and made available, for our pleasure or torment."

(Also, by providing visual indicators, the froth serves as a marker to reveal the quality of the preparation, which is a line of inquiry worth revisiting, which we plan to do when we reconvene, to investigate the matter of absinthe louching.)

"Coming next are myrtaceous embraces of eucalyptol and walnuts and crackers and kiwi fruit ... then rosaceous traces of benzaldehyde and vanilla and *piloncillo* ... then a finishing flourish of grilled potatoes?"

Thank you, I'll have another.

Perfumes of Allurement

On this day we continue to unravel a string of thought, about perfumes *de la naturaleza*, about the dimensional communicative capacities of such organic expressions.

"Cranberries paired with pistachio?" Saffron has lately been engaged with molecular pairings.

Take for example, abstract art or mass media for the most part, or commercial perfumes … their activity is linear, they drive and spin with the same orientation, affect us on a single plane, reach us from a certain approach, come at us from minimal angles, don't bombard us from every direction upon multiple tiers as do Earthly etherealizations.

"Salmon with liquorice?"

Even a great concerto won't simultaneously soothe anxiety and calm inflammation and dissolve kidney stones too, as some essential oils will do. Even a Van Gogh oil on canvas doesn't have the facility to serve medicinally and sacramentally and socially as a psychoactive agent and perhaps a cosmetic and an aphrodisiac too, fulfilling the numerous actions concurrently, as some aromatic extracts do.

"Yet there's more to it."

The catalogue of provisions is book-length, but those self-referential lists test our failing patience. In any case, it's clear that plant perfumes are in the metabolic big business of multiplex agency among humanity.

"Oranges with butternut squash?"

We are presently scheduled to take up the assertion that perfumes are all potions of seduction.

"There is the idea that diesel fuel is erogenous to someone who consummated a love affair in a garage (we don't buy it)."

Many claimants insist reductively still, that the endeavor of perfumery, as performed by people, concerns carnal union exclusively (whether it's unmistakable or understated, outright or insinuated, whether it's witting or unintentional, out-and-out or subliminal). They remind us that perfumes consist of sexual secretions of flowers that often mimic pollinator sex phero-mones, or emit fecal notes that trigger ancient memory traces (of the good old days) of genital inspecting, mutual genital scru-tinizing among primates.

"How biodegrading."

And they remind us that perfumes are constituted also of res-inous exudates with elements structurally similar to animal ste-roids, hence stimulating neural remembrances of pheromones passing with urine. And they remind us that perfumes also include ingredients of fixative substances that are poached and pirated or plagiarized from mammalian attractants like musk and civet, which strike chords that are ammoniacal and nitrogenous.

"That's a fantasy, that modern perfumes incorporate genuine and authentic metabolites from tropical blossoms and tree ducts and glands of animal anuses."

Of floral volatiles, beetles track those fruity or aminoid. Bees and moths and butterflies follow trails of saccharidal scents. Bats respond to emanations that are fruit-like or musty, or occasionally to rank methyl sulfides. Flies go after chemical expressions that are downright excretory, such as those issued by aroid plants.

"Hawthorn blossoms flaunt a fragrance similar to that of vaginal emissions."

With respect to our study in sensuality, we're blending a furtively yearning aroma oil for designation as an aphrodisiac elixir. How is the exercise going?

"Our Tanzanian geranium oil functions prominently to impart a genitalic cheesy nuance, and a small amount of Virginian cedarwood distilled from heartwood provides the preparation with ratherly steroidal resin alcohols."

I detect early inviting vapors of clove and cumin? then tuberose and ylang, to arouse? patchouli and vanilla, labdanum and tolu balsam are each scentingly suggestive in their own way … what else, to provoke erotic desire?

"A stingy pinch of orris butter with its myristic acid confers the odorful allusion to prolonged intimacy in the bedroom."

It displays something foxy and estery like methyl anthranilate from mandarin, and something indelicately indolic also shows up, perhaps that's jonquil, or broom or cassie?

"It lets off something lactonic or apiaceous, which may be lovage, which is an imperative in any witch's love-brew."

It projects something ethereal and venereal, or rather like sweet cereal spilled on a fusty carpet, or like the musky carpet lining an athlete's armpit?

"It's not *Levisticum* but celery-seed extract that supplies some of that nutty ketonic androstenone, held falsely as a human pheromone but nonetheless olfactively connotative of some erogenic hanky-panky."

The sour goaty fragrantness ... I figured we would attribute it to spikenard? and the pubic-hair reference ... I considered it owing to a smidgeon of terpeneless cypress?

"Those fleshly principles are subordinate to adorning terpene molecules in unrectified cypress essential oils."

Finally, styrax is incorporated to characterize the drydown, its hydro-cinnamic alcohol expressive of the perspiration that results from activities usually carried out in private?

Perfumes of Magnitude
(Thyme)

Saffron taps spoon to wine glass and guests immediately heed, "For a change I now introduce our salon leader, who will speak (can't stop) of genuine perfumes of Nature that waft from genuine plants and carry genuine messages of Life."

There's a coffee drink named after me, at *Cafe Super-Bien*. The proprietor says that in each pod is a trace of a Nepalese super-critical carbon dioxide extract of cardamom and a few beans picked from the feces of Vietnamese rodents.

"Next, your Salonnier is to speak generally about specific concrete things which we experience locally and personally."

I'm peeved about the troubling fate of Creation, and the widespread flattening out of natural variation, which is attributable to the modern way of seeing and dealing with the World. So I'm offering a depiction, with a modicum of irony, in the style of cookbook recipe, this one for accruing wealth and control, a sort of gastronomic reduction.

"Instructions for how to prepare a *soufflé* for success."

To begin, you reduce an intricate whole conception of a complex phenomenon to its parts, discard all situational non-generalizable pieces of your understanding, all novel and idiosyncratic particulars, to leave only a stripped down set of components suitable for formulaic reassembly. The parts should be interchangeable from place to place and time to time so that the recipe can serve as a template for myriad operations. The previously nuanced totality is now perfectly reproducible, primed for flawless duplication... proceed to duplicate... repeat the steps over and over ... straightforward enough? Surely you'll appreciate how your efforts are exponentially more encompassing, like nets that are cast more widely, how your reach is extended and your influence is amplified.

"Come forward onto the bandwagon—watch your step—there you go—everybody up."

Congratulations, you're a modern-world success story. Your concoction can now be dished out again and again—unchecked by Earthly impediments—variously elaborated while retaining your standards—to bestow advantages with no foreseeable limits.

"Congratulations, you've become infected. A virulent contagion has you endlessly abstracting in the style of a relentless horror-film zombie, mass-producing artworks and technologies and stories and businesses and merrymaking and sex, and filing for patents and trademarks, then passing on the germ."

But wait, since over one billion burgers have been served (the decree of an iconic example, an early archetypal pioneer now long superseded), the students of the super-mechanism are surpassing the teachers with new approaches to renounce organic awareness, new ways to ignore the state of Nature, new means to disregard Earth-based reality, new ways to deny their biological heritage, new strategies to tune out the voices and neglect the voiceless of the biosphere.

"Inasmuch as the new achievers still pursue prosperity, their endeavor, as before, is subject to numerical organizing principles that, as before, are based on fraudulent assumptions and shrouded subsidies and concealed costs."

Now, our cookbook reduction needs only to be broken up, such as the breakup set in motion with the atomizing advent of the Internet, and you have a new round of iterations, perhaps even more de-Natured than the last, owing to the late-surging spree of scattershot virtuality.

"The recent tide of ad hoc innovating is surely no less Earth-negating than the generalized undertakings that came before."

Though the cross-promotions and interlocking interests are perhaps lately less direct and obvious, financial instruments still reign, and corporate ventures continue to accrue power, shaping vast dumbed-down deracinated artificial environments packed with anti-Life messages.

Did we mention the character of commercial perfumery? which offers a universe of cookbook reduction so vast and elegant as to be allegorical?

"Okay, that was a wordy preamble in anticipation of this evening's flights of volatile oil. Thanks for oiling the works, for our work with odorful oils. So who among our panel of pundits shall lead off?"

"Biting and herby and campfire-smoky—pungent and piercing and hospital-soapy—like foliage of sage and rosemary mostly."

Are you referencing thyme the idealized botanical icon? or thyme the cohort of metabolizing beings growing somewhere out there? on hillsides or outcrops or coastal plains or woodland edges or among scrubby brushwoods (*tomillares*) of southern

Spain? If the latter, we should acknowledge the full constellation of evolutionarily restless taxa, including forms and populations we refer to as wooly thyme and common thyme, cretan creeping lemon and garden thyme, caraway mastic and minor thyme, tufted tuffet magic and tiny thyme, silver-hair and mayfair thyme, tea thyme and mother of thyme—

"Thyme has long been considered an herb of courage, probably due to the assertive anti-infectious properties," Saffron interrupts my recitation.

I was just getting started, thought we'd learn a thing or two about morphotypes and cultivars and vegetative sports, selection and phenotypic variation, that sort of thing, also the tangled practice especially in Mediterranean regions of cross-assigning the appellations savory and oregano and marjoram—shall we? not interested?—never mind then.

"Neovitalist Paul Lee says that his favorite word is the Greek *thymós*, which can be defined as something like a Life-affirming kind of courage? a courageous aspiration? an aspiring spirit? a spirited vitality? He associates both the thymus gland and the herb thyme as bearing out the meaning of the term."

Sooner or later, we'll need to confront the chemical polymorphism head-on, to recognize the numerous so-called (by the European phytomedical faction) biochemical specificities, also called chemovars—chemically distinct though morphologically indistinguishable subspecific groupings whose chemotypical development usually owes to epigenetic changes that are shaped by growing environments—eesh, thyme taxonomy is, well, let's say we just skip it?

"The somatic region of the thymus gland, he fancies as a thymic field, where reason (mind) and desire (body) are bridged."

[74]

But supposing we were to stage a streamlined review ... we'd need first to recognize a number of distinct species, these mostly of fiery phenolic composition, for instance: Moroccan thyme (*T. satureioides*) boasts a prominent fraction of borneol along with some carvacrol heat. Another, called serpolet (*T. serpyllum*), is contrastingly distributed across northern Europe while especially characterized of hot constitution due to its high concentrations of carvacrol. And another, referred to as Spanish thyme (*T. zygis*), is centered on the Iberian Peninsula, and again, is disproportionately identified by its spicy germicidal principles (as indicated by many analyses of marketplace thyme oils, which are derived mostly, albeit often opaquely, from variations of Spanish thyme).

"The gland is located just below the chin, in the upper chest."

There's more ... in the pertinent literature, there is some sloppiness of interchangeability with another species-level category that's commercially important: garden thyme (*T. vulgaris*) is a western Mediterranean taxon renowned for the circumscription of distinct chemotypes, chemical forms denominated after the molecules predominantly expressed—with regard to the sweet types, those are terpene alcohols, namely geraniol or thujanol-4 or alpha-terpineol or linalol—the phenolic types are likewise designated, distinguishable by phenols pronouncedly present, namely carvacrol or thymol.

"So he opened the Wild Thyme restaurant in Santa Cruz. They served sweetbreads of thymus glands as the house specialty."

But wait ... we should also note that, whereas this infraspecific classification applies to both wild and cultivated plants, the clusters are often reinforced and intensified by willful selection and clonal propagation, as commonly practiced in southern France by artisan distillers. Wildcrafting, on the other hand, is potentially an exercise much less precise, incorporating more diverse assemblages of plants, which in cases of fuzzy delimitation may collectively be assigned the appellation *population thyme*, the essential oils from which are usually more complex.

"Lee also planned to market a healing salve, which he would call ... thyme balm."

Hold on, now ... in the matter of so-named red versus white thyme oils, it appears that there is no want of ways to misattribute the distinction—iron versus onyx distillation retorts? improvements by rectification of the skin-aggressive distillates?

"*Dermocaustic* may as well be an aromadermatological term."

Definitionally, the white oil is a red redistilled, but that's rarely the case, which most buyers realize (since the secret hasn't been well kept, about the commoditization involving falsification and compounding).

"Still it's confusing, because the adjectival red is sometimes used in counterposition to white, in which case it should signify a product unmanipulated, but sometimes used in counterposition to sweet, in which case it should signify a phenolic oil, the strong stuff?"

Put plainly, the rusty-hued commercial oil may be derived, at least in part, from existent populations of *Thymus* (most likely Spanish thyme), but as for those shipments labeled *white thyme* ... of naturalness there's a slim hope, of authenticity not a ghost of a chance.

"What you perceive is what I perceive, which is the thymol type issuing a provocative tide of herbaceous effects with a teetering tinge of camphor, and also a trace leads us to infer menthol but it's probably by our association with other ingredients of disinfecting formulations."

Garden thyme gathered in Provence yields one and a half pounds of oil per ton of plant material, while Spanish thyme from southern Portugal and Spain yields thirty pounds of oil—from the same amount of plant material (after so-called readjustment, of course). Figure that.

"The carvacrolic samples evoke a focused fragrant presence that is forwardly, practically piercingly thyme-like? thymish? thymous? thymaceous? thymic?—the dry-away is dry all the way—the dryout is dry all the way out—the drydown is dry all the way down."

Adulteration is most likely to entail the addition of cheap synthetic para-cymene, sometimes thymol or alpha-terpinene, occasionally fractions of ajowan or rosemary or pine. The altered and rigged compound may not even incorporate a drop of anything extracted from plants we relate to that phylogenetic entity ... genuine thyme.

"Gives off a cloud of zest like a spice-exhaling shade of dusty piquance?—it could be *za'atar* in a jar left in a hot car—also shows a muted tanned-leather aspect—as it volatilizes, the aromatic vapor becomes coarse and rustic as it shifts to approximate without ever achieving woodiness?—flashes a sharp sensory impression that's burnt but not tarry—for the term *phenolic*, Spanish thyme is the type specimen to anchor the defining olfactive features?—comprises a suggestion of a disguised expression which implies a sensation derived from medicated cough syrup?"

Perfumes of Engagement

"In *narcotráfico* terms, *levantón* refers to a forced seizure, while *secuestro* indicates a kidnapping, the *levantado* not likely to be seen again alive, the *secuestrado* though standing a chance, often pending payment of a ransom."

Our reference library of fragrant dilutions is housed inside three large refrigerators, each by night wrapped with a cable strung through the handle and secured with a bicycle lock. There are borosilicate glass bottles of twelve or twenty-four mils seated sixty per basket, in rows separated by paper stock partitions on two tiers of customized stainless-steel stackable trays.

To transport everything, the uncommon bounty of volatile oils and equipment, Saffron and I drove with few breaks, making it across the border without event. The sun was low in the sky as we neared our destination, however our sighs of relief were premature…

"So now, the traffic slows suddenly, a military roadblock ahead. We figure, this is not for us a lucky turn."

Reaching the barricade, there are four trucks *de la Marina* and a bunch of soldiers wearing ski masks and holding AK-47s, gesturing with their rifles to pull over, to exit the vehicle, to stand where they designate, the weapons pointing at us (is that really necessary?), as they want every box and container unloaded, and all glassware unwrapped, and packing material removed (are they kidding?), so we begin to open the cushioned and encased flasks, the beakers and nebulizing diffusers, the pipettes and hoses, they say to work faster (should we be concerned?), the shaky table is quickly crowded with logbooks, digital scales, filter paper, rice ash, mica plates, wooden spatulas, porcelain censers, waterproof inks, aroma-expansion chambers, perfume-testing *mouillettes*, bamboo charcoal, they say everything should be brought out (they're not pleased), resinoids and spices, tinctures and distillates, high-proof alcohol and other diluents, solvents and solubilizers (we're not pleased), they ask about the glass beads (we use them to minimize headspace as solution levels drop) and about the heating mantle (it's part of the distillation apparatus), next Saffron brings out our newest accessions, a chamomile from Chile and a hyssop from France, uh-oh now they begin to dump all the brimmed scintillation vials onto the table (I'm trying to stay unruffled), they want us to remove the vessel lids (seriously?), they ask about this and that extract, about the Croatian rosemary, the several citrus from Argentina and the Australian bush oils, they want to know the cost, the utility and provenance, *el costo? para que? de donde?* here allow us, no we don't sell these, (still speaking through the mask mouth-holes) they ask how we support ourselves (eesh).

"And, well, before we realize, we're presenting a workshop, a few *aromathérapie* tricks we have cached to our memory, to verify our harmless eccentricity."

Aquí tiene, sample this ginger, this grounding primal fire, when life is chaotic (like now) spread the oil across your foot heels and arches, blow-dry and then apply, or here, on a cotton ball, keep it, *de nada*—this neroli elevates and encourages, use a drop when a hint of despair threatens, plus its indole component stimulates fleshly animal energy—coriander too is mildly euphoric, go ahead and pass around this infused blotter strip for others to regard—all right, try this, a spot of Mitcham peppermint administered on the tongue for stomach upset.

"So ... during this demonstration, the soldiers all slowly make their way over to us (their dispositions otherwise are hard to read, their faces still concealed behind masks)."

Aquí, we've been this spraying myrtle *hydrolat* into our long-drive tired eyes, you try—and this next is inula the miracle mucolytic, inhale slowly—okay now, marjoram is a heady touch, notice your environment seems like an echo-chamber, anyway it's short-lived, no worries—here's a dose of Roman chamomile, the queen of antispasmodics, it's a powerhouse soporific to decelerate after your methamphetamine binges, to break the fall (a spill in our vehicle and we'd never make our destination)—hyssop conversely is stimulative for driving through the night, thwarts depression as well.

"So ... after a time, we notice ... their weapons, no longer aimed at our heads."

Perfumes of Heritance

Nice to be back, to once again experience that signature national perfume of horse sweat and woodsmoke.

"There is no place like a home base, in any case."

I've been reading about some local personalities, the ones that bury little girls alive, thrust ice-picks in people's throats, kidnap kids to harvest their organs. They go by names such as El Chango (the monkey) and La Ardilla (the squirrel) and El Toto (the pussy).

"Those monikers would be funny if it weren't such a matter of life and barbaric death."

In this locale, where criminal *narcotráfico* is still the unofficial central organizing principle, a *sicario* signifies a hitman, trained by practicing with a sledgehammer or machete against someone tied up. But if he doesn't perform well, he may hence be designated a *halcón*, a lookout.

The nature of people around here is to be submissive (except for when they're not) (except for those that aren't).

"...whoosh, pass the message—oils containing the sesquiterpene beta-caryophyllene are scattered, by which we mean distributed scatteringly, among the diversity of plant phyletic lineages, in that this metabolic courier endows biotic perfumes with a dusty dry rendition of the lively blown candied clove tone, less clear and creamy than the eugenolic version but spicy and tenacious, so we follow the molecule as it breaks away from entangled notes of Somali frankincense where its role is minor, hitchhiking with green lacewings and banana weevils, corn rootworms and brown loopers, to embrace associating chemical principles among ambient vapors around plants of black pepper and marigold, ylang-ylang and patchouli and cannabis along with kindred hop plants, eventually to mingle with emanations hovering around a community predominated by a Chinese nepetalactone-poor chemotype of catnip, where it intermixes with—psst, pass the message—"

Much as the *narcotraficantes* develop innovative ways of killing people, they also resurrect bygone methods, like crushing them under cattle hooves, decapitating them with saws, cooking them alive, sometimes inside barrels of sodium hydroxide, until they become like soup.

"Massive inequality, the prevalent condition around the World, is interpreted variously by different cultures. Each society has its own slant on injustice and abuse."

Apparently an important criterion is to prevent any shred of dignity at the time of death, so underpants of the slain are pulled down, genitals sliced off and stuck into the victims' mouths, these sorts of things.

"...whoosh, pass the message—the volatile terpenoid ketone d-carvone, notably enantiomeric with a minty mirror image, which furnishes the distinguishing scent to caraway fruits and imbues also a select other few sweetly herbaceous botanical perfumes such as those issued from dill seeds and mandarin peels wherein the distinctive spicy-pickled warm-oily seedy-bread theme is incorporated, albeit frequently only in traces, inasmuch as even emblematic caraway plants sometimes invite just a moderate carvone contribution, for example certain populations in Egypt which are dominated by—psst, pass the message—"

There are a couple of familiar *narcos* indicated to be imposing types, who are played up as El Talibán and El Tyson, and who, we gather, are generous with messages of public interest, as for instance, that recently provided by the one who goes by El Ostión (the oyster)—it's a tip on how to dismember someone—

"...that you should always strangle the victim first, before you begin cutting off body parts, so that blood won't spray and splatter all over the place, which would ruin a carpet."

In keeping with such a drift, they are also known to boil infants to death, in front of the anguished parents, in oil-filled vats designed for cooking pigs. One at a time, the little babies would fit into the cauldrons.

"...whoosh, pass the message—the sesquiterpene germacrene-d, which adds unobtrusive woodsy-verdant accents to many hundreds or more discrete forms of Life throughout the biosphere, to cockroaches citruses gingers pickleworms chamomiles mints carrots myrtles and on and on, and to the lingering nectareous fragrant face of heady headspace borne by mature blossoms of ylang-ylang trees and influencing the molecular messaging of melissa and birch bud and tea rose blossoms, and anise herb—muah, pass the message—"

You'll soon see that, as a relatively weighty compound, germacrene-d joins the full complement of its chemical compadres late in the distillation process, imparting effects to those fractions of ylang-ylang more reluctant to take flight, you'll see.

Perfumes of Flux
(Honey)

⁓◦⌇◦⁓

"Tonight's salon owes to the labors and favors of bees," Saffron announces her entry.

We don't romanticize, rather, we recognize, or rather, we lionize the signal-rich yet blatant direct dances of honeybees.

"*Asistentes* get set, and go," Saffron sets the occasion in motion.

Scent samples of *miel* tinctures and *cire d'abeille de Francia* products are already passing around, "heady nectareous heavy and sweet showing glowingly mellow like soft subdued heat is this waxy warm genuinely natural conceit like the wagging and circling dances of bees, in phases these layers lay out a buttery basis neath a smooth oily handful of fine herbal powder and straw bales and strawberries for a grassy impression of fumes that are slightly funky and lightly smoky meaning they exude volatile molecules that summon the senses and fire reminiscences of offerings smoldering in censers coated with resins that are notably nipping like the evangelizing vapors this extract is emitting, presumably it's phenylacetic acid transmitting the flirting visiting serving of felinity, or let's say, it makes a display of something like caramelized sugar and urine-soaked berry-fruit glazes with olive-oil-soap-like traces, or let's say, it's a spray of perfume fixed into a pair of unwashed leather pants?—after wearing by an unwashed woman?—ja-ja, but with respect, this aroma reflects sex—or let's say, the effusing bouquet is evoking the feeling of a tacky scratchy mattress whose filling is infused by a choking cloud of diffusing tobacco exhaust created by the chain-smoking of bidis following multiple uncomfortable turns of intimacy in a hayloft, explicit enough?"

Awkward.

The golden rich solvent extracts of beeswax and honey often correlate with the bees' sources of floral nectar, be they lavender locust mesquite mint or citrus, sunflower aster *huisache* sage or eucalyptus. (In the matter of distinct varietals, it is nearly unbelievable how they're clearly perceivable by accomplished perceivers, by those devotees of diverseness who severally treasure the creamy or liquid or comby or chunky elixirs from Nature.)

"Elixir, from the Arabic *al iksir* which is from the Greek *kseron* meaning medication."

(Snipped here are ten minutes of aimless discourse, leading to my becoming exercised):

I haven't intended to make mention in this session, that honeybee symbolism deals with oppression, that it leans politically leftward, given the tireless gathering by bees of nectar stores to benefit the collective and all. But now I feel triggered to turn to a style more polemical and less hypothetical, as we take up the matter of how people respond to any given chemical. It is hard to ignore all the platitudinal talk about the imminent fashioning of some type of predictive system for gauging our responses to infochemicals, including the enigmatic perfumes of Life, expectations publicly related by Nature-averse followers of reductive perfumery, who appear blind to the inscrutable range of variables that influence subtle metabolic affairs and deep indwelling senses, who seem inattentive to the vast asymmetric hodgepodge of chance fluxing factors involved. Achh, my headache returns as I consider the disordered gamut ... how both subject (the beholder) and object (the fragrance) change from moment to moment: of the former, there is psychological disposition, pattern of breath, circadian and other physiological shifts, olfactive acuity and age of receptors—of the latter, there are perpetual changes of constituent profile, as components undergo chemical reactions with each other and with neighboring metabolites, comprising for example infinitesimally nuanced substitutions involving functional groups, as a few electrons bump from one molecule to the next, to sometimes further incite a cascade of reactions. The settings in Nature of such transactions fluctuate too, like temperature and humidity and air currents and other such fluid conditions.

"To reproduce a Nature-made fragrance? is like a musician in a studio trying to reproduce a memorable live performance (slim chance)."

Still, to conceal their true program, the chemically venturesome rely upon cover of the notorious recent-era divorce—we're referring actually to actions, to agency, to acts ... how the actions of actors have been distanced from the actual effects of those acts ... in other words, the disconnection between deeds and consequences, between human affairs and their repercussions. The two sides have become systematically separated to such an extent that it's frequently impossible to track trails that mark courses of causation.

"That's a provision to advance the purpose-driven mission being prosecuted against Creation."

Recently, for the first time, after more than three and a half billion years of Life on Earth, the originating agents of disputes mainly remain behind the scenes, their identities shadowy and obscure. This bears heavily on the chemistry of Life, as during just the few recent decades, a hundred thousand new compounds that have been promiscuously introduced into our environments are now stealthily slipping through ecological webs, having biological and aesthetic effects many miles and many years removed from their sources and causes of derivation.

"The Fragrance Industry is not moved by the plummeting state and fate of biodiversity."

The more brazenly phytophobic among the dealers and make-believers in perfumery maintain that there is no such thing as natural, that the state of Nature doesn't exist. And the fraudful fraternity denies even the most obvious strikes against vulnerable beneficiaries of Nature's services, say, for instance, frogs with their genitals mutated owing to the xenobiotic activity of synthetic molecules developed in order to fulfill the ideas of trend-faithful designers.

"Those are neomanic ambitions of technophilic estheticians of organic chemistry, who are anticipating opportunities to realize their mission, to give material Life a makeover, to materialize their vision."

Perfumes of Constitution

With today's introduction you'll be tutored in the critical analysis of perfume by the exercise of an entry-level aesthetic encounter with an exemplifying fragrant agent of Life, an envoy making contact in the first language of Nature.

"The native tongue, favorite medium of communication, primal messaging system of Life."

Awaiting you is the substance and reward of becoming fragrance literate, by which we mean aroma astute, by which we mean scent smart, by which we mean that you'll learn to make sense of your experience of bundled infochemicals, being metabolic messengers bearing manifold meaning. You'll learn to mentally organize a world of sensual qualities, to develop a skill set for sharp sensory beholding, to evaluate activities and functions of perfume and to interpret transmitted ideas and attitudes, exhibited views and values, to relate percepts to concepts by which we mean that you'll learn to recognize odorful forms that derive from feelings and thoughts.

"All right, our sample extracts have been prepared. Let's position ourselves to draw the vapors into our bodies. With our eyes closed, we inspire, slowly, three times, no more no less."

Now: what do you infer? what is first referenced? connoted?

indicated? what next? and then? what is revealed and what remains concealed? is a degree of tension expressed? conflict? pacification? and the reactivity? the intrinsicality of distinguishing character? the rate of transmission? the scope of the effusion? the properties of presence and diffusivity? of radiance and expansivity? of *sillage* and substantivity? and the footing and focal point? the *note de tête* and *note de coeur*? foundation and exterior? undercarriage and core? complexion and structure? bouquet and base? the highlights and associated factors? accents and enhancements? adjunct nuances and tones? is each note essential? are components buttressing or fleeting? and the nature of the drydown? its tenacity or duration? what do we mean when we speak of the perfume's scale?

Saffron addresses some class bellyachers who are quietly grumbling, "The *anuncio* read: you'll require no special skills or experience for this workshop, only the welcoming reception of your sense perception."

That's right, for example, in the case of my proprietary scentful compositions, beholders impressed have remarked that I must have a special aptitude, a keen olfactory ability. I respond by insisting no, that I smoke cigarettes, that my nose-hole is usually stuffed, which is hardly different from a painter having tired reddened eyes.

"An inspired painting isn't a function of the artist's keen eyesight."

Continuing: are top-notes purged of terpenes? diluents employed? is the menstruum filtered? clear or cloudy? are certain fractions cast widely? and others vented lightly? does our subject aroma inspire a sense of integration and unity? equilibrium and proportionality? does it impress as exalting? flirtatious or bold? where does it fall along a graded divide from symmetry to imbalance? refinement to raciness? congruity to discordance? buoyancy to heaviness? openness to entanglement? from eliciting a mood somber to gay? and the temporal evolution? does it modulate or diminish or degrade with maturation? and its behavior on differing substrates? does it mellow in its flacon or on skin? adapt or harmonize to a setting? to a user's aura?

"They say that a chameleon perfume is a tiger and an ass and a pig and a nightingale, that you never know which will show up."

Continuing still: of our blend, did the composer work with chemical context and scented scenery? surroundings or framework? which fragrant factors are denotative and which are implied? which are up front, which are behind? paraded or illuminated? are the constituents internally cohesive? do they tend to consolidate or differentiate? are dissimilar elements bridged? can you identify the theme? the fore and the background? does the perfume unfold according to a running narrative? what aromatic aspects are dynamic and what are stable? and what odor families are featured? represented? what about lineage and affiliations? any social context you can imagine? do you make out any ideals asserted? sensibilities supported?

Next up, Saffron and I have planned an exercise for the class: she challenges the panel initiates, "Salonists, shall we have a respite and shift gears? to put to a test, your facility of olfactive discernment? your clear-sightedness in the range of odorousness?" So first, she passes around a *mouillette* imbued with tobacco absolute, and we suggest that the percipients be mindful of certain aromatic principles—sweet fruits and animal feces, facets of castoreum and dried apricots and old dry ashtrays. Then following, Saffron distributes a blotter strip bearing the same exact extract yet labeled as another distinct, and this time we direct the students to regard discrepant features of the fragrance—of leather and hay, abutting notes of honey and figs and mellow cigars. So guess what? surprise surprise, they fall for the trap, with no idea of it, no clue that the two were actually one, happens every time.

Perfumes of Severance

"Shall we begin?" Saffron begins.

This evening we entertain with a modest investigation into the physical basis of perfume.

"We're just now getting underway."

Sometimes the serene weighty atmosphere of these salons recalls for me a traditional Japanese *kodo* incense ceremony, what with all the exercises of ponderousness.

"We'll begin momentarily."

At other times these plant perfume panels resemble a noisy free-wheeling with-elbows-flying ritual feast, calling to my mind an unruly Jewish Passover dinner I attended once.

"So latecomers, please find your seats."

In between aromatic flights, to combat olfactory fatigue, we refresh our palates with freshly squeezed lime juice. Or we breathe deeply through wool scarves. Or inhale roasted coffee beans. Smoke cigarettes. Eat salt. Sip on vinegar. Do deep knee bends. Take brisk walks outside.

"Ready, set, don't go yet."

There was previously a panel member who would inhale through silk panties, remember? insisted that was most effective to clear olfactive clutter? He eventually moved on to accept a lucrative job in the Perfume Industry. We weren't surprised.

"Now, we're waiting to bring this ritual about."

Shortly, Saffron will speak to our group about the transnational concern, International Fragrances & Flavors, that sent roses into space with the shuttle Discovery.

"That matter is not off topic."

But first, I'd like to lay out the thrust of this instruction with a round of graphic demonstration, to make sure the gist is not missed.

"We're sitting up and standing by."

Imagine: heaving a bucket of water-soluble dye over a waterfall ... it disappears by dilution, yes? and then, hurling a bowling ball into the rapids ... zonk, it sinks by gravity, no? but then, throwing a table-tennis ball into the same torrent ... bingo— in this illustrational model, the ping-pong agent would negotiate its surroundings in a manner that is comparable to how lightweight molecules (good volatility) travel independently (limited reactivity) and readily spread out (excellent diffusivity) yet don't much interact with water (constrained hydrophilicity) in the watery World of our residence. How very well-suited physiochemically are such bitty oil-friendly metabolites to serve as the leading messengers in Life's primary messaging service?

"The diminutive compounds are as large as Life."

We are Earthlings, biologically fine-tuned to physical parameters here on Earth. Ancestral events have been captured in our body cells and tissues, better preserved than photos could ever be, perpetuated as composition and form and function. The salty aqueous substance that flows within us is a record of our primordial marine past. The big transition of Life from ancient seas to colonize new dry regions is ingrained in our being. And the millions of years of diversified experience on land is reflected through and through, the epic evolutionary pageant all recapitulated, on our home planet, the seat of our Creation.

"Life is too short."

Way way back, when an early membrane fragment folded, wrapping in upon itself, into a closed shell, the separation created an interior environment distinct from everything else outside.

"The origin of individuality."

About these membranes in history ... individual organisms would benefit by the partially hydrophobic layers of tissue among the water-based solutions within, for as they are non-dissolving, the laminal structures could serve to divide and compartmentalize, contain and direct the movements of substances, to control and facilitate metabolism.

"So, we're set for life."

More about these membranes ... they are largely lipidic, therefore they are welcoming to lipophilic molecules, namely the tiny transmissible fragrant principles of low polarity and high volatility that don't agglomerate, the infochemical couriers that are so well suited for travel among air currents—the membranes and missives are mutually affiliating, chemically congenial. So you see, the membranes are vital to vital beings, serving to detect external signals in the cardinal operation of communication among the living—that is, to receive and read and reveal the meaning of perfume.

"The most primitive and elementary dance that has ever been danced is the dance set in motion by the most primitive and elementary means of contact among forms of Life."

Again, about these membranes . . . we can now appreciate why essential oil droplets floating on the surface of bathtub water will cling to an exposed body constructed of cell membranes. So we should issue the warning to be careful when bathing. What we are saying is that undiluted oils can be bracing, and aggressive oils will substantially irritate skin.

"The dance of Life is the dance inspired by perfume."

Continuing now, this relates to membranes . . . the quintessential dichotomy of oil versus water, this is a little misleading . . . and construing the polar dyad as mutually exclusive, this is a misreading. For example, a longer hydrocarbon tail improves a fragrant molecule's solubility in lipids, which usually signifies that it will have a stronger scent, and you can see, this influence is realized by measure of degree.

"Western society has the appearance of an expanding web of prosthetic devices? with no shades or grades or limits within sight?"

And fat-loving molecules don't associate much with others of the same, not in the way that water-loving (polar) compounds grab on to each other (by forming hydrogen bonds), but this too is a matter of degree.

"The quest for money and power and prestige appears among the deniers of Life to never let up? seeming unequivocal, never measured?"

Adding a gram of pure vanillin into a cup of water for blending, no problem. But attempting to mix into the water a much larger amount, this invites challenges of miscibility. The flavorful compound is considered lipophilic, yet with a modicum of hydrophilicity. Its chemical behavior rests on the state of proportionality, its solubility assessed as a matter of degree.

"The Earth-averse agents of reduction and control are never satisfied? Where is the hedging?"

Odor manifests as a matter of degree, lipophilicity as a matter of degree, chemical polarity as a matter of degree, solubility as a matter of degree. The agency of perfume is a matter of degree. Our affiliation with Creation is a matter of degree. The violations, evidently, not always so.

"Overnight Scentsation is what they named the rose."

All right, returning now to the subject of that astronautical rose cultivar ... we are led to acknowledge how very many are drawn to future scenarios involving space travel? and I don't mind saying that I won't mind waving bye-bye, bidding farewell (with a wink) to such deniers of organic reality. I won't mind helping them to load their spacecraft, as they'll surely have lots of massive equipment to haul.

"We'll call it Starship Biophobia."

We won't mind saying and waving bye-bye good-luck (wink wink) to all such who entertain extraterrestrial fantasies.

"And then, we won't mind hanging back to feed ducks, pick dewberries, collect rainwater, breathe over blossoms, run from snakes, swat mosquitos, and make compost."

Perfumes of Inquiry

Our salons resemble more a circus than a form of worship, and appear now to function as a social function, to an extent as a coming-out event, or a form of theatre, our program of exercises fashioned to feature captive clouds of storytelling principles in Nature.

Blotter dipping strips are imbued and reviewed by our minyan with opinions, "This oil is lemon petitgrain, afraid to say that it dispenses a suggestion of something leaking from a dishwasher like a dryish dispatch of dishwater."

Between fifty and three hundred species every day are rendered extinct forever.

"It issues an etherealization with a well-integrated presence like a reference to some mature chord, maybe lime juice is reflected or asparagus neglected in the back of a fridge."

The estimate of biodiversity loss varies so widely because species in the tropics are wiped out faster than they can be catalogued.

"Though undiluted, this next sample of etrog citron is nonetheless muted, yielding a suave smattering of vaguely terpenic and estery character compounds like citral and neryl and geranyl acetate."

We happen to live across from the rear entrance of the *perfumería*, by which I refer to the entire mazy dwelling, but the perfumery proper is only a small commercial space, its storefront hardly visible from street view and facing away from us. In any case, we have the vantage point from our rooftop terrace lookout to see the large interior *laberinto*.

"There's a little commotion now and then, vehicles moving in and out."

Whereas the entirety of the quarters is too artless to be considered a *palacio*, there are various courtyards, unfinished construction, different parking areas, and a loading dock where shipments of fragrances are received.

Strips dipped in lemon are now making their way around the table, "Of *citronnier* rind oils expressed, the South African is tart, the Sicilian is oily, the Spanish is squeaky-clean, the Uruguayan exhibits a verdancy augmented by a fine midsection that is near albeit clearer than a may-chang interior—and this next brusque vapory piquancy is a zest perfume from the Kingdom of California?—this one, from southern Italy, effuses a bed of clean laundry or lemon ices or fizzy soda, idiosyncratic by the way it releases trickling terpenes succeeding the leading ozone-breathing metallic-seeming volatiles, giving the whole impression an appealing brand-new feeling ... the attributive *tang* is probably most apt to refer to the distinctive toppy brightness (for those unfamiliar with the term, this essential oil exemplifies a lifting lemony telltale tanginess)."

On the *perfumería* front facade there is some signage that's barely visible from the road. However, on the back gate there is a double-M wrought iron insignia displayed, which stands for

Matadores de Maldad (slayers of evil), the trade name they've adopted ... according to Saffron.

"I thought I earlier heard muffled sounds of screaming from inside—ja-ja just kidding."

On any given day, among perfumes loaded on pallets, such as *Kouros* by Yves Saint Laurent and *Signature* by Donna Karan, there are ten to fifteen trucks and sport-utility vehicles parked within their gate. None have license plates, which I'm told is insignificant, indicating nothing.

"Salonnier, your headaches, they may be due to your anxiety, or your burdened conscience. Still and all, they are more likely induced by toxic vapors originating in the fires of brickmakers."

Am I the only one concerned about what goes on inside the *perfumería*?

Perfumes of Accounting (Gardenia)

"Evening greetings. In these proceedings we're scheduled for revealing and we'll touch on the meaning that we take from another aromatic substance with a sketchy past involving forgery," Saffron welcomes our guests.

We're not quite ready to initiate tonight's flights, so we'll set out, per our ritual, by sharing some thoughts, maybe to inspire a notion, stir up some commotion, beginning with the question:

"To what is our experience of volatile oils owed? (how shall we justify our love?)"

These essential oils strike us as heavy heady harsh or harmonious by virtue of their precise chemical composition? as creamy clean catty or cloying due to the nuanced ecological affairs of their biological sources? as faint foul fishy or floral by reason of the genealogical heritage of those source plants? as lush lactonic leesy or leafy owing to the fluxing situational way that shrubs trees and herbs issue particular fragrant metabolites in response to environmental conditions?

"All the above, and more…"

On one hand, plant perfumes are products of communities.

On the other, phyletic lines of descent. On the first, responses to economic challenges. On the second, enabled and constrained by biosynthetic machineries contingent upon genetic heritage. The realms of ecology and genealogy crisscross and overlap to shape the scentful system of communication that's featured among Living Nature (a simplification, sorry).

"And more…"

Or, in order to explain our feelings, shall we focus on the receiving end of the transaction? Shall we set our sites on the beholding side of the equation? and take up a detailed study of the science and psychology and metaphysics of hominid olfaction?

"Moreover…"

In any respect, living beings react back. Associations evolve as individual lineages evolve, entailing contextual yet unpredictable courses of negotiations among and between plants and animals and people. Our perception of infochemicals isn't a one-way function, nor is it straightforwardly prescribed by genes, rather it results from interacting suites of senses shaped by intersecting suites of relationships. So, you can appreciate, our investigation gets more complicated by the moment.

"Moreover more…"

Also, compounds modify and transact with each other diversely when heated and cooled, stored and shaken, blended and subject to abiotic elements such as sunlight and humidity. There are oxidation and hydrolysis reactions among other molecular rearrangements, even fermentation takes place, and glycosides (as in celery) or glucosinolates (as in cabbage) are tied up and sometimes released upon enzymatic cleavage (we'll avoid, for now, the subject of how different metabolites are generated, say from carotenoid degradation and lipid oxidation).

"No more!"

And, cultural factors greatly influence the way aromatic principles are brought into being and slotted for perceiving. Say, the specificities of making selections and farming, of distilling and transporting, of the various fluctuating nonlinear pathways by which fragrant extracts make their way to the places and times of their impressions upon us, of all the contingent yet asymmetric and unforeseeable economic and social interactions and events during the passage, regularly involving producers or brokers— the same considerations apply?

"What began as tutorial is now oratorical," Saffron solicits affirmation around the table but receives mostly bewildered looks.

And what of all the ways that environments impinge upon captive volatiles? the sundry impacts that are independent of intrinsic properties? Say, touching up by vendors, hot conditions of warehousing, artifacts of distillation, random contaminants, perhaps from residues in storage vessels...

"Earlier you were educating, now reiterating."

I'm nearly finished: what of poorly understood non-genetic developmental influences within plants? Theoretical biologists publish papers about interiority, the effects of internal constraints or piloting?

"Before this was a worthy endeavor, now it's a wordy lecture that threatens to go forever."

I'm, errr, very nearly finished: to account comprehensively for the vast fragrancy in Nature, regarding correlations that bear on causation and throw light on our sensations, among metabolic affairs we partition shares to forces Darwinian and—

Saffron cuts me off...

"It has been, for a time, nearly impossible to procure an actual Earthly expression of this. However, there have been botanical doppelgangers about, pleasing evocations crafted with jasmine sambac and other white nectareous flowers, with spicy tropical references contributed by coconut and cardamom, for verdancy perhaps touches of galbanum and galangal, and for milkiness I suspect a trace of butter extract."

I gather our review of gardenia begins now.

Classifying floral fragrances is a knotty mission. Delimitation is often based on the extent of spiciness versus rosiness versus presence of ionones. Most schemes also recognize a white-flower group, exemplified famously by jasmine, narcissus and honeysuckle too, and gardenia.

"These white blossoms characteristically emanate sweet heady chemical dispatches that cater foremostly to hawkmoths."

In the matter of perfume, the sphingophily is unmistakably material if not all-explaining. In such, the nectar may not be easily attainable, deposited at the base of a tubular corolla or floral spur, which can serve as an anatomical clue. And given that many of the lepidopteran pollinators fly by dusk or night by the manner of hovering in the air, blossoms that lack landing platforms are adaptively matched, serving as another potential indication of moth visitation.

"We're now to be joined by the dispersive waftings of *tiare* as they give off memory-prompting vapors of cinnamon and honey and remindful flavors of chocolate and vanilla and faint recollections of hyacinth."

That's a sample of a Tahitian (Polynesian) *absolue* derived from flowers of *Gardenia tahitensis*, an ambassador from the coterie of kindred gardenia, yet a taxon dearly distinguishable from its congener, the cultivated icon *Gardenia jasminoides*. Also, there is a nice coconut-oil infusion in the marketplace that goes by the name monoi (but beware when ordering, many exports are extended with preservatives and tainted with a phony fragrance).

"Radiates especially green and lactonic—intimates ylang-ylang—integrates wintergreen and tuberose—shows off shades simultaneously medical honeyed and earthy—finally drying away with layers feigning feces."

The white-flower category is loosely defined by a certain molecular syndrome, for instance benzenoid esters (benzyl acetate, methyl benzoate) and nitrogenous volatiles (indole, anthranilates) are common, terpene alcohols too (linalol, nerolidol, farnesol). Then, within this faction, distinct chemical contours further distinguish themselves, as in the case of gardenia, by the generous transmissions of beta-ocimene and some tiglic acid esters and lactones.

"Jasmine lactone gives a creamy faint peachy paint milky effect, which is to say, a *Cocos* character, which is to say, a denotive display of the lactonic quality, which is to say, the suggestion of a baby's breath right after feeding?"

In any case, the redolent putative gardenia material that chemical suppliers have been peddling all these many decades? can be summed up in three words—synthetic styralyl acetate—a single molecule that has approximated, more suitably than any other, in all its leafy weed-seedy green-fruitiness, the targeted ambience of the gardenia seeker's desire. This compound has been employed in myriad commercial perfumes, with the routine assignment to bestow (however cynically) a dryish lifting floral facet summoning (however incompletely) the full aspect of living gardenia headspace that so resists impersonation.

"A solvent extract from China is also circulating. It connotes maybe some balsamic candy fading to aromatic molasses, an odd accord, so much so that we might suspect real bona fide naturalness?"

This next is an ambrosial *concrète* from France, for which authenticity is supposedly guaranteed. All the same, we find that this waxy paste is a little familiar, even faddy as it comes on olfactively fatty and then caramelic and green, in the manner of, sorry to say ... styralyl acetate.

"Once again, thieving dealers have taken us naive dreamers to the cleaners," Saffron repeats the familiar rejoinder.

Impressively, there has become available a genuine extract (*Gardenia fragrans*) from near Bogotá, Colombia. While the traditional solvent of tallow and lard is replaced there by palm oil, otherwise it appears that the producer practices straight-out enfleurage?

"The same extractive facility is also giving tuberose the treatment."

The thermolabile flowers are picked and laid out across glass plates secured by a frame (chassis), wherein they emit scent principles for a period, the dispensing volatiles received by the lipo-inviting oil, which is recharged with fresh flowers until substantially suffused (the saturated menstruum is now a *pommade*), next comes alcohol washing (yielding an *extrait*), and lastly the concentration of perfume by the removal of alcohol under vacuum at low temperature—*voilà*, inimitable absolute of enfleurage (and the *pommade* is sold as so-called gardenia butter).

"Surprise—though the aroma delicacy was out of stock, we have a minuscule dollop sample, scraped from the side of an empty vessel and sent to us from Colombia, as a favor."

"Upon release it serves up a metabolic bundle that is lightly herbal and slightly delicate but turns faintly fungal and vaguely greasy—this is a hint anisic in a syrupy cordial-like style not unlike simple syrup and suchlike simple signals—the oleaginous edge has a complex complexion, a spot sensual and intoxicating, rich and narcotic—the effect is oily, perhaps due to a solvent residue?—yet the fatty flourish is apparently an inherency, not artifactual—the sensation spans from my pharynx all the way down to my—"

How shall we account for this? this sensuous bounty? that so privileges us? these sublime portfolios of Nature?—and the designer responsible?—our understanding of the sequence of anteceding steps to produce such a thing?

"It lets out an effusive diffusion of a diffusing effluvium, about as refined, I find, as scented toilet paper—with respect?"

As guest panelists draw the molecular messages in, into their bodies, their recognition of our expressed curiosity unfolds. The questions we've posited gradually ring more true for them, as with each breath they experience some puzzlement and awe . . . exactly, our offbeat inquiry is legitimized.

"We haven't just been blowing air."

Perfumes of Depiction

"Today's salon, to spotlight sandalwood, has been postponed."

Why is there yellow tape draped around that house on the corner, near the *libramiento*? no cause for alarm, you say? but what are the *federales* doing there? digging up the yard? searching for victims who will remain unidentified, as usual?

Never in my life.

"...whoosh, pass the message—the phenylpropene ether e-anethole issues an inimitable accord of subliminal saccharidal mimosoid elements to umpteen plant species including sassafras cinnamon oregano juniper myrtle marjoram osmanthus michelia and celery, even magnolia flowers, love bugs and honeybees and rose chafers too, while in larger concentrations it bestows the prototypic warmly medicinal pungently candied lively anisic olfactive character to some basil hyssop tarragon fennel chervil and star anise, and anise seed (but not to liquorice, the historic confection traditionally made from roots of the leguminous herb, and which is the subject of a confusing circular association), also it finds room among hundreds of other metabolites agglomerating within vaporous headspace layers of Bulgarian rose blossoms renowned for complexity of constituent profile where it joins with—psst, pass the message—"

The love of life.

In *narco* terms, *poco a poco* refers to a gradual method of torture whereby an unfortunate tied at the shoulders is *poco a poco* dipped with a winch into a fifty-five-gallon drum of boiling water ... revived by a doctor upon fainting from pain, then *poco a poco* lowered again ... as the physician ensures that the victim is conscious each time the body is *poco a poco* lowered. During the process the cooked appendages are *poco a poco* incrementally cut off.

"... whoosh, pass the message—the terpenoid ketone menthone, a diffusively fresh dry minty molecule that adds a refreshingly dulcifying mentholated highlight to roses, while skulking among other similarly minor constituents, including many monoterpenes that stage a bonanza of influences in the shadow of the more prominent compounds therein, namely citronellol and geraniol and nerol, as dashes of this impactful cooling principle also understatedly enliven the bouquets of scattered populations of angelica frankincense combava thyme and some lemon trees in Japan where—psst, pass the message—"

A mission in life.

Another *narco* torture method is enacted upon a captive who's naked, *todo desnudo,* bundled up in a blanket or thin carpet, *se le pone la manta,* which is doused with gasoline and then lit on fire. In not too long the covering is pulled off, while still burning, so that the skin comes off with it, then gas poured on the raw exposed body. They say that the intensity of pain defies any description.

"... whoosh, pass the message—another isomeric molecule, the monoterpene d-limonene, predominating constitutionally though not aromatically in citrus fruit zest oils, imparts a relatively thin and volatile odorful effect, characteristically airy-light and lemony-brisk, and terpenic of course, sweet-tart-toppy without much body, it dilutes and envelopes (almost like a carrier or a menstruum) the big-footprint fragrant foci of oxygenated terpenoids, and appears also as scant fractions of insect semiochemicals (spangles beetles aphids ants engravers stainers weevils borers termites and stinkbugs) and countless (really, too many to count) plant emissions, some emanating from communities of Finnish summer savory—muah, pass the message—"

A kiss of Life.

Perfumes of Temperance
(Champa)

First, I digress.

"It's not a digression, strictly speaking, more like a preamble, the sort delivered without further ado," Saffron says.

Then, I reflect—that botanical perfumers, against those who boastfully wrangle with laboratory-derived single molecules, have defended their idealogical turf by analogizing a homemade apple pie made with natural ingredients to a store-purchased artificial rendition.

"Seems a proper and pointed comparison?"

The commercially processed pie is pumped full of potent synthetic flavors to compensate for the tasteless old apples, while the authentic indulgence is a creative yet very limited (simple) culinary arrangement of wholesome (complex) organic materials, of derivation close to their Natural World origins.

"Cinnamon nutmeg and sugar, apples wheat and butter."

Aromancers are privileged to channel Life's impenetrable sublime splendor, to sponsor evolutionary masterpieces that are beyond emulation. In the case of our delicious rosaceous dessert pastry (mouthwatering *strudel de manzana* included), the apple and cinnamon alliance reveals a prototypic flavor accord in Nature, a metabolic proto-harmony, a model partnership of fruit and spice.

"The aromancer's restraint of cookery accommodates immeasurable intricacy from the kitchen of Creation."

Already, strips of perfume-imbued paddle-shaped blotter cards are rounding the long table, so the reviews begin:

"This absolute radiates a quality oh-my-god rich and exotic as all get-out—exhibits within seconds a body that's sweet suave and heavy and velvety and getting very heady already—the mellifluousness evoked is warm and refined in a singular way that's difficult to break down—it recalls some scent to our senses, not that of tuberose, not ylang, not jasmine, whereas those are data points."

All that, inspired by the experience of a single drop of oil?

This evening our organoleptic initiation will be brokered by several fragrant samples coaxed and captured and sequestered from one of two congeneric species, trees we've previously considered as *Michelia* but are now deemed by a recent taxonomic revision to be magnolias.

"We're living life by the drop."

The yellowish-flowered progenitor (*Magnolia champaca*), golden champaca, native of the temperate Himalayas, probably India, these days to be found all over tropical and subtropical Asia, upon enduring hydrocarbon solvent extraction encounters our sensory reception evaporating from a liquid embodiment that is sometimes coined champak extract or absolute.

"One drop will fill you up."

And the white-flowered successor (*Magnolia x alba*), often known colloquially as michelia, of smaller stature, a sterile hybrid never naturalized in the wild, having probably originated in Java or thereabouts, surrendering fluid expressions designated champaca oil and readily available from China in the form of carbon dioxide extracts, arrives to make our acquaintance today as a diffusive outburst blasting off from the *mouillette* like a battery of shells or flares targeting the olfactory tissues behind our nares.

"One drop will fill the room."

There are attars from India as well. The dedicated artisans there are still at it, incorporating chemical principles into the referential matrix of sandalwood, contextualizing the effusion and modulating the transmission of featured volatiles over time.

"We have at least a drop of the essential oil too."

This oil is distilled from michelia leaves (that's the white-flowered taxon). My take? It throws out a forthcoming fine toppy linalolic inundation against a sustained background ambience of cellulose and lignin, which some liken to petitgrain and perilla and others to tulip and fig foliage (to point up the differences in the inferences), followed by the emission of references namely to anise and tea leaves (to point up the ignition of remembrances), then comes a lasting grassy structure that's oily and herby to a degree, all the while a chord of clary and rose plus lavender is being issued, much as it persists in the gradually fading bass clef.

"And there's an essential oil from flowers."

But the essential oil is not procured directly from blossoms. The solvent extraction comes first and only subsequently does the dense *concrète* become subject to the entraining steam vapors of acquisition.

"A drop remains, maybe more (again, from white, not yellow, blossoms). This oil is another that's linalol-rich, and precociously verdant before becoming midriffy like floral wax or honey, then mutedly indolic, recalling the robust flower power of orange flower."

We're thankful to receive this next glop, which is less than a drop, let's say a droplet, of the absolute…

"Early on we're aware of a dry faint florality, owing perhaps to the ionones, or the esters, or the jasmine compounds. Then the impression becomes intensely lush and sultry, recreating the perfumed atmosphere of humid oriental tropics, with molecules of indole and methyl anthranilate involved in the odorful action. And also grassy herbal helpings of cis-hexenol are served, and there's a smooth effect like gentle waves of woodiness, presumably due to the sesquiterpenes."

Pollination of flowers is sometimes rough play, especially when the invitees are beetles who jostle in a feeding fracas after having been lured by widely wafting creamy-lactonic or fruity-ethereal vapors. These scents of solicitation comprise predominantly esters such as methyl butyrate, which gives a pineapple presence with banana backnotes, and methyl 2-methylbutyrate, which has a hand in the fatty green-apple sensation. Plus, para-cymene imparts spicy hesperidate character to the welcoming bouquet. Altogether the system of signals induces frenzy in coleopteran visitors who are rewarded for their stopover with a potluck offering of stigmas and pollen and nectar secretions.

"The champaca carbon dioxide solvent extract is complex, with facets recalling spikenard, or muguet—or an imitation of carnation, or cumin—or bringing to mind something like wine, something fermented—or some kind of cultured dairy dish—with an apricot topping or something resembling, the ingredients being hard to get a fix on, though not necessarily rare, like say vanilla, or say pear—or say oxidized lemons, there's staying power, no question."

I anticipate a query but choose to skip the commentary ... the answer is yes, adulteration is customary, a marketplace reality.

"In the matter of champa incense, we offer a workshop upcoming," Saffron announces.

The champa in nag champa is derived from champaca, whereas the nag in nag champa is derived from nagarmotha, the aromatic sedge.

"Granted, synthetic odorants are commonly used, and the familiar Satya Sai Baba blue box has little to do with the botanical material of our interest, but all the same, there are many mixtures and interpretations, many renderings of nag champa incense. Halmaddi resin (from *Ailanthus*) is a common constituent, and other components include olibanum and benzoin as well as vanilla and cinnamon and saffron."

Perfumes of Wonder

"How shall we justify our affirmation of the goodness of Creation?"

Living is more than just mechanical, fragrance is more than the physical sum of well-defined chemicals, and plant perfume is more than just a simple signal. Empirical intricacy to the point of immeasurability is among the indicating markers of authentic Nature.

"How shall we defend our partiality for Earth-based reality?"

But incomprehensibility to the point of unfathomableness is the ground into which seeds of supernatural forces are planted. Taking cover behind cloaks of channelers or conjurers, finding refuge among the divine or occult, resorting to koans from mysticism, casting anchor in the palliating safe harbor of abstract deities and metaphysical explanations, we're sorry to say, means eschewing the Natural World.

"How shall we explain our regard for biotic perplexity?"

When experience reverts to mystery, when explanations revert to questions, when science reverts to poetry, we'll know that we have nearly arrived. When we fathom that our analytical tools, neuronal tissues and powerful computers, can't grasp the full scope of information relating to Life, we'll know that we have very nearly arrived. It's Life's elegant paradox. And we have already arrived.

"How shall we stand up for our adherence to verse over prayer?"

Very well, by those opening remarks, we're led again to the absorbing terrain—the recognition and interpretation of perfume. And I can't resist taking up the detailed propositions of emperor you-know-who regarding primary odor perception, as they're so befitting and elegantly musical, yet I need to hold my *nariz* while reading.

"How shall you rationalize being seduced by a biophysical hypothesis that's been soundly refuted?"

First, please indulge this excursus, but I wonder if our disposition to ravage everything wild and free is not innate? but rather, some sort of bewitchment engineered by hard-core hominid counterfeiters of Creation? more nurture than nature? a subtle psychological condition? a trance-like possession? by which our conceptions of Life are corrupted? smothered under a cultural blanket of hypnotic me-mine-our messages? or an occult spell of solipsism?

"If so, such a spell has been cast widely, having influenced many men of letters."

Emperor-of-scent Luca Turin for example, an alpha-humanist *hombre* of the universe who can't help but lust after odorants unknown to Life, a deluded savant of sorts, estranged from organic reality, perhaps having absorbed a good share of the sense-numbing fairy dust sprinkled about by biophobic operatives of the impostrous Perfume Industry these last dozen decades?

"Also Turin's partner, the phytophobic *nez* Sanchez."

According to Turin's neurobiological theory, within a given chemical compound, atomic bonds can be likened to elastic springs formed by the frenetic whirling of electrons to hold together atoms, the springs vibrating at particular frequencies depending on functions of atomic weight and bond strength, each bond like a tiny swirling electrical necklace ringing a particular note, resounding at a particular pitch, with a particular wave number, and the sum of bonds sounding a particular molecular chord, a composite vibrational fingerprint.

"The bond between hydrogen and nitrogen vibrates 3,350 times per second," Saffron reads from her class notes.

Do you make out how tiers of such activity are nested in Nature? how electromagnetic elements continually combine and interact? at successive levels, to form structures horizontally and vertically compounded? how each substance endowed with such energetic elaborateness is thus a composition unique? often immensely involving, impossible to transcribe? how vibrational chords come together over and over again in the ecosphere to make a kind of signature song? the reason we compare the nature of this ceaseless system to the layering of music? to orchestras communicating with orchestras? symphonies transacting with symphonies? why we put forward such illustrative depictions to convey the idea?

"The bond between hydrogen and oxygen vibrates 2,900 times per second."

Of course, this form of energy isn't audible (with ears) or visible (with eyes). And parenthetically, insofar as they make up a fraction of the grand vibrational pageant of our sensory experience, music of sound can be turned away with ear plugs, and displays of color excluded with blinders. In contrast, spinning electrons perceived by our olfactive sensors are not rejected so easily—if we value being alive, we had better remain receptive to these emissive mechanisms within molecules ... since we receive them with each breath.

"The bond between sulphur and oxygen vibrates 2,500 times per second."

So, we don't deny it, that our favored big-picture consideration of this perfumed planet is enhanced by the assertion that the complexity of composite atomic interactions spikes higher at new levels and ranges of organization.

"A big production."

Individual atomic bonds are grouped together as fundamental components of individual molecules, which in turn are grouped as oils sequestered in ducts or glands or other chambers within plant tissue, which in turn are released into air and grouped as headspace vapors skirting particular parts of a plant, which in turn are grouped to constitute volatiles blanketing a broader area around the plant, which in turn are grouped more ambiently to disperse around the vicinity of the plant, which in turn merge as effluvia carried away by currents and clouds of air saturated with the fragrant fingerprints of countless living beings.

"So enjoy the show."

Considering all that an area of perfumed atmosphere comprises—the humming atomic bonds within volatile chemical compounds, within metabolites specific to given plant organs, within vaporous emanations specific to given whole plants, within emanations specific to given assemblages of neighboring plants, within emanations specific to wider-ranging plant populations, within emanations specific to animal and plant communities—can anyone imagine the complexity of the spectacular scentful euphoniousness that rides a countryside breeze?

"With your eyes closed, stand in a grassy meadow and inhale, and appreciate how it's impossible to adequately put your sensation to words, how it seems hopeless to make any mental sense of the fragrancy, which is somehow related to honey and hay and cherries, but more. Much as you get the point, you find it difficult to account for the point that you get?"

If single atomic bonds reverberate at particular pitches or tones, then at successively wider-ranging levels of organization, tonal complexity increases exponentially. So the single sound that rings from a particular rope of whirling electrons combines with others to compose a molecular chord which combines again to compose a composite chord which combines again and again to make concerto encompassing concerto which perfumes environments with the primary back-and-foreground chemical music of Creation.

"It's a metabolic extravaganza with an ensemble cast and numerous long-running plotlines."

All right, this compulsive play of metaphor construction has exceeded our allotment, yet the analogizing serves figuratively for our purposes, to help portray the aromatic action? of messaging metabolites blazing courses through increasingly complex chemical environments? So, with permission, we call your attention to a first-chair cellist who joins with a second-chair cellist, the duo in turn joining with others to constitute a string section, then a chamber orchestra, then a symphonic orchestra, then other such orchestras, the dueling and cooperative music makers relentlessly suffusing Earth with the polyphony of Life.

"It's a dramatic rendition of the tragic form with elements of dark comedy."

Next, allowing that this may puff up the exercise a touch, still we should point out the process that leads to collective behaviors: we note that, of a compound, the OH (hydroxyl) group has properties that individual H (hydrogen) and O (oxygen) atoms lack, and that CH3OH (methanol) molecules similarly have properties that individual OH groups lack, and so on. This real-World manner of development—in which each new level of organization hosts an improvisation featuring new properties, new molecular personality traits, new chemical idiosyncrasies— is designated by the term . . . *emergence.*

"Multiple meanings take up multiple levels."

So, yes, perfumes of Nature reveal a superlative display of emergence, elegant to a supreme degree. Emerging attributes are realized upon constituent interactions (inter-reactions) involving atomic bonds of combinatorial arrangements, in that, at each new hierarchal tier, vibrations newly acquaint with one another. So, yes, downstream qualities of fragrant metabolites may offer shapeshifting-like surprises, having unfolded in chancy dimensional ways that are less linear and additive while more asymmetric and opaque. No one can map out the tangled chemical choreography of Life in advance, as the precise tonal harmonies and molecular dances are resistant to analysis, influenced by too many variables (so, yes, it hurts my head to try to tabulate the possibilities).

"The theatrics concern friends and enemies and lovers."

But . . . fragrance chemists in the business, we're sad to bear witness, of remaking the World to their liking, have ticketed Nature's ineffable expressions for describing, Nature's incalculable representations for deciphering, Nature's indeterminable transmissions for dissecting and eventually foretelling. In order to accomplish this, they've been working tirelessly to seal up the wild open systems of biospheric Life.

"Pasting and plugging up the World, with adhesive to subdue, and caulk to control."

It's a reductive ritual common to physicalist laboratories everywhere, to tease apart the enigmatic aspects and trim down or purge the innumerable subtle traces of organic Life, to diminish the breadth of natural variation so that chemical changes become predictable. In time, we fear, they'll achieve some success—innovative technologies will more-and-more reliably foresee an emerging fragrance. But only in the contrived world of their making, not the control-resistant World of our biological origins.

"Tension doubt conflict revelation consequences resolution or catastrophe?"

An extract of Bulgarian damascena rose bushes hydrodistilled in the Struma Valley subtly emits wave vibrations of tens of thousands of atomic bonds. Upon early proliferation of these expressions, the rose aroma is unquantifiable ... with later surging, unqualifiable.

Perfumes of Foreboding
(Camphor)

We now resume our period retrospection.

1643—In England, association between perfumery and healing is reinforced by pharmaceutical vendors who also sell aromatic waters for non-therapeutic applications. And in France, association between perfumery and lofty social status is reinforced as King Louis XIV renews the Perfumers Charter and institutes rigid rules of admission to the select profession, including requirements of four years apprenticing followed by three years in a kind of probationary role.

1708—And, the aura of elitism is reinforced in London by Charles Lilly with his exclusive enactment of the well-known storyline concerning celebrity perfumer among high society, his shop (nice collection of scented snuffs) serving as a meeting place for the literary and fashionable (to be succeeded by other perfume apothecaries, for instance those established by Bayley and Floris, later Yardley, and in France, Houbigant and Lubin).

1719—Early stirrings portend changes approaching? In Europe there's a surge of interest to study volatile oils, and drawing a great share of scrutiny are phenomena of fractional congealing at lower temperatures and glaze-like coatings and particulate secretions on leaf surfaces. Such observations will hold the attention of researchers for decades.

Caspar Neumann, working in Berlin, notices a certain separating and sorting behavior in the form of coalescing crystalline deposits among constituents of essential oils, namely those of thyme and cardamom and marjoram, and is beckoned to identify the single chemical component disassociating from the context of the whole. He designates the congealing chemical as camphor.

"Our present interest shifts..."

Neumann is followed by others who isolate similar compounds that they too call camphor: French chemist Geoffroy (1720) looks at crystals of sage among other oils, Dutch scientist Gaubius (1771) separates colorless precipitates from peppermint oil, German chemist Wiegleb (1774) examines crystalline substances in mace oil, and Spanish scientist Arezula (1785) finds like materials in lavender sage rosemary and marjoram.

"To the coroner's lab bench?"

Investigators will eventually elucidate the respective correct identities of these volatile metabolites characterized by relatively high congealing and melting points. The compounds will prove to constitute a heterogeneous group of chemicals, not just the singular ketone that will later become widely considered as camphor.

"The pathologist's autopsy table?"

It's a historic time, we now recognize—integral aromatic oils are manifestly composed of parts, and the enterprise of enumerating the chemistry of Life has been inexorably embarked upon ... in full swing ... no going back. The full set of Nature's molecular expressions is being lined up for investigation, each to have its turn on the dissecting tray.

"The vivisector's counter?"

1798—The campaign's frontline combatants welcome a weapons upgrade—vacuum distillation—by which reduced pressure allows the separation of oils to be carried out at lower temperatures. Much as this appears, on the face of it, to be a benign, even promising, means to protect the labile and fleeting constituents of fragrant vapors and thus defend the integrity of whole harmonious plant exudations, it is, however, developed along with corresponding methods for fractionation, and so the two operations come to be commonly administered in tandem—termed *vacuum fractionation*—useful to purify, more or less, metabolic principles that are otherwise signaling only upon commingling within perfumes of the Natural World.

"The necrophiliac's altar?"

(The privilege of hindsight affords us the revelation that this technology is not so harmless, rather more like a loaded gun in waiting.)

1816—The press is on to extricate recently discovered molecules from their entanglement. Benzaldehyde has already been discovered in bitter almonds, and vanillin is newly isolated from cured vanilla pods. The infatuation of humanity with reductionism, with the practice of reduction, is in its early phase.

"Remember your first crush?"

(Who had any idea of what was coming?—who could have predicted? that large-scale institutions like big-agra big-oil big-pharma big-infotech and big-perfume would bear such big enmity toward anything little, anything local and limited, native and primitive, innocuous and passive, the vulnerable by virtue of being diminutive, and that they would develop such big plans to implement big designs to roll out big guns to prosecute a big siege to be laid to Creation?)

"The onslaught is presently looming."

Perfumes of Overture

Do you doubt that artifice has captured the imagination of our human kind?

"You know, I'm not exactly normal, since I don't care for belly laughs or dancing, shopping or even romancing, preferring instead brisk walks, obscure literature and intellectual talks," Saffron says.

We live in an age of virtuality.

"I would never serve or wait on a man, not for his phone call or approval or promise of commitment, or gifts of chocolates or lingerie."

Humanity is punch-drunk in love with virtuality. And the associated orientation of endearment with respect to abstraction has been dominant for some time. The more virtual, the less concrete, the more universal, the less particular, the better. The face-to-face and one-at-a-time approaches to negotiating this World have been abandoned.

"I'm not the family type, not the woman to accompany you to funerals or functions, or stroll with you hand-in-hand, but I have an untamed side and it would be nice if you acknowledged what I mean by that?"

The more generalizable the better, the fewer the outliers the worthier, which is to say, things more predictable are preferable, things more unconditioned and unifying, formulas proofs and doctrines, models and patterns and programs.

"I don't pray or meditate, don't practice intuitive healing or yoga, don't fret mistakes, and would rather you not harbor so many expectations?"

Guiding threads and global markets, common purposes and organizing principles, the eternal mantra and the *aum* of God's name, spiritual enlightenment and ultimate redemption.

"I don't give tantric massage yet I'm able to maintain the interest of a man, and it would be nice if you appreciated what I mean by that?"

The divine event, embracing vision, undifferentiated one-ness, single element, fundamental law, supreme truth, theory of everything . . . congratulations, your affirmation entitles you to wealth and salvation.

"I've never had time for courtship, love, or marriage, won't try to explain as I'm not sure you care? In any respect, it would be nice if you didn't requite my revelations with disapproval, we'll see."

Actual Earthly organic substances under attack by intan-gibility?—such imagery may or may not help us to spread the message effectively, but we surely can and should pro-test that Life is under siege, and there's nothing metaphoric about it.

"I admire unambiguous expressions and I believe you know what I mean by that?"

In trouble . . . things that have originated and developed, and have been shaped free of human plotting, are in trouble. Things that are vital and vulnerable, as well as the real-time one-on-

one exchanges and interactions between such living breathing beings ... are in trouble.

"I realize that you're drawn to Nature, but you give the impression that your precise orientation is still in flux? by which I refer to your worthwhile determination backed up by your labile resolution."

In trouble ... species communities languages cultures and ecologies are in trouble. The fabric of Life is in trouble, frayed and torn more each day, and the various distinguishing features of Life ... are in trouble.

"I've followed you, Salonnier, to this place, yet I admit that I'm presently a trifle unsatisfied with what we're doing here, answering a call to battle that is anything but clear."

Do you doubt the urgency of our endeavor?

"I take seriously and value our work, captivated by perfumes whether of seduction or decomposition, which you may find strange, I don't care."

(Soon after these appeals, Saffron asks whether my singular unrelenting pursuit is that of developing the philosophical narrative in my head, to the detriment of my reliability.)

"Forever challenging, never engaging?"

(And I begin to wonder whether she expects me to change so that I'll better conform to her ideal of how someone should go against adversity.)

"I can imagine myself becoming your biggest problem, or my collaboration could be the best possible solution to the challenges of your inquiry, it just depends."

Perfumes of Conscience
(Myrtle)

It's a worthy endeavor, to stand on behalf of collapsing fisheries and coral reefs, wetland ecological communities on the brink, natural habitats on mountaintops being mined, to stick up for environmental refugees or others trapped without options in urban ghettos.

"Myrtle shrubs grow wild in Turkey, Algeria, Tunisia, Spain, Italy ... the pattern is evident enough—all around the Mediterranean, leaves and twigs and flowers are distilled with steam to yield a pleasing dewy spicy volatile oil with an outdoorsy (just enough) cooling property."

It's rightful to make noise about people working desperately in faraway sweatshops, subsisting as if caged animals, or to testify about the sentient animals themselves suffering indescribable abuses in massive industrial farms, or about offenses inflicted by biotechnology concerns.

"This red oil sample circulating, under natural light it looks more amber?—the distillate strikes me as effusively vibrant, brisk and alive, full of youthful top-notes yet to become disillusioned as occurs so often in middle age—its activity cuts fresher moments delayed upon the blotter strip."

I fear, all the same, that our exploits are lame.

"The as-much-as-possible approach is to align as much as possible with those aspirations we hold most dear," Saffron says.

In this regard, we should refine our ability to make out artifice where it turns up, such as to distinguish the aroma of a boreal orchid from that of a petroleum-based Nature knockoff, a pristine woodland ecosystem from a managed parkland, a thriving urban community from an intentional theme-housing development, a genuinely righteous person from a crooked evangelical proselytizer, an eatery generated by passion from another inspired by a business plan, a small artisanal Burgundy from a widely traded brand of wine, an indigenous subsistence fishing ritual from an industrial operation, an unmanipulated specialty aromatic oil from an industrial commodity.

"The whichever-way-is-feasible approach is to affiliate in whichever way is feasible with those causes we most believe in."

There used to be a convention among military firing squads in which one of the several shooters, without knowing it, was given a blank bullet. Thus each member could believe that his was the harmless fire.

"It's an old whatever-it-takes custom, to use a whatever-works technique, handy to serve the executioner's psyche."

Of course, we do as-much-as-possible in whichever-way-is-feasible to get along without moral burden. However we do it, we do it togetherly, as cooperative psychosocial effects such as the diffusion of responsibility help us to carry on resolutely. Let's say, the curtains are neatly draped so we're screened from seeing the assaults carried out on our behalf, wouldn't even know which way to turn in order to confront our victims, to face the consequences of our unthinking actions?

"No single raindrop thinks it caused the flood."

By docile conformity (intended demoralization) or informed cooperation (wilful blindness) or total surrender (voluntary submission), we march in step (we creatures and creators) to the repetitive drumbeat (we conscripts and commanders) by which ineffable expressions of Life (vital particularities) are dismantled and replaced, we (subjects and administrators) follow the program, which, among other things, calls for the creation and dissemination (indiscriminate provision) of new test-tube innovations (xenobiotic introductions) not to mention the advocation of the chemical desecration of Creation.

"The situation of our time surrounds us like a baffling crime," I recognize the quote.

We flounder, entangled within a Nature-despoiling anomic social order, overwhelmed in cages of co-optation under blankets of bureaucracy weighing down, as if we're paralyzed because our shameful secrets are communal, our hands collectively dirtied.

"It's a common crime syndicate or gang initiation ritual, having new recruits carry out a brutal slaying, so they reach promptly the point of no return."

We're in this together and no one will be caught holding the bag, due to a lacework of interactions, so challenging to unravel, of constant deadening deals that secure our place in the grand insidious scheme.

"Sierra Leonean rebels and the Sicilian *mafiosi* and Mexican *narcotraficantes* each press initiates into murderous service by indoctrinating rites of passage."

With getting dressed each morning, then breakfast, then our drive to work, we become complicit in the plight of destabilized faraway communities, of bleak isolating land developments, packed freeways, petrochemical farming, falling water tables, depleted soils, climate change … all this and our day has just begun.

"Some of us choose otherwise, to go the way of Mennonites, or draft petitions, compose songs, feed and house our fighting partisans. Some may choose an insider track, or teach, or write letters to editors … or administer plant perfume salons."

With synthetic odoraments, we can hardly help but anoint ourselves each morning. By simply bathing and adorning, shaving and performing many other such commonplace acts, we find ourselves conforming, joining in the defiling of emissive Life, which is for me a most disturbing complicity—the daily ritual patronage of the cult of promiscuous chemistry—given that this symbolic service to our proprietary swollen cephalic tissue is also a slight against the molecular messaging issue of Nature.

"We are treated this evening to experience, then to share our private inferences, concerning a perfumed delegation representing two recognized myrtle chemotypes…"

The red type is not always but usually produced in hotter regions like Morocco, asserting more 1,8-cineole and piney-residue notes and terpinyl acetate, this latter principle eliciting wads of woods and waxes empowered by herbs and flowers.

"There is an accord or a chord in its core that connotes not so much myrtle as allspice and something herbal, more of a gastronomical enhancement than a myrtaceous complement— the bouquet becomes evanescently sugary upon its drydown dissipation."

The green type is toppy while exhibiting more refinement, or so they say, a Corsican specialty for adherents of *l'aromathérapie*, transmitting more myrtenyl acetate which radiates fresh green and cooling, and linalol which intimates a soothing florality and a glowing orangeness recalling *bois de rose*.

"Much as it throws out a presence of camphorous and cineolic elements, this sample taken from the green group spotlights a linalolic essence, with scarce allusions to citrus, then eucalyptus, hyssop implied, fennel traces peeking around, cedarwood too, against a seedy underpinning and fruity backdrop, both understated."

Perfumes of Continuity
(Basil)

"With eyes closed, we home in on subtle accents, herby rosemaries and punchy phenols, woodsy eucalypts and spicy carnations," Saffron is advocating on behalf of our featured extract, considered in Hindu tradition an archetype of Hindu femininity.

"Within your roots are all the sacred places of the world, and inside your stem live all the gods and goddesses, and your leaves radiate every form of sacred fire, tulsi, you are mother of the universe," she reads from Vedic scripture, which is not known for restraint of poetic expression.

But the holy tulsi of India is only one of many dozens of species and subspecies of basil, the designations of which are innumerable. Even taxonomic botanists have been bested when it comes to straightening out the craggy eclectic roll call of names.

"We have sweet basil, exotic basil, Reunion basil, estragole basil, African blue basil, Thai lemon basil ..."

There is a sarcastic adage that experts of systematic nomenclature explain things by making them unintelligible, and this warning is especially applicable to assignments of disentangling knotted cases of cultivated plants ... basil, for instance.

"The inexplicable is earmarked."

The taxon referred to as basil includes many variants of interest to fanciers who move plant stocks around, which is to say that plants become displaced from their native ranges, and so phyletic indications from local floras get lost, the relational clues no longer available to taxonomists.

"The incomprehensible is cornered."

And new environments invite adaptive modifications, which are prone to become exaggerated since visible changes are subject to intentional selection by breeders, and favored phenotypes are also promoted by people unconsciously. And then botanists must also reckon with new hybrids, accidental and deliberate, new mutations sports forms lines clones, achh—it can be a messy business, plant systematics.

"The inconceivable is concretized."

Yet it appears for sure, that no matter all the dizzying diverseness within and between factions and congregations of basil, still basil is basil—basil is basil is basil still, see? No matter the interspecific hybridization, no matter the floating discontinuities, no matter the blurry interfaces—no matter the threat by variation to chemical and morphological and aesthetic unity— still basil is not rosemary is not spearmint—yes no? There's a basil-ness to basil that's absent elsewhere in Nature—no yes?

"The unfathomable is realized."

And, much as cohesive subdivisions of basil plants are sometimes found at different taxonomic levels (cultivars varieties species), the genus basil remains still forever basil—it makes little difference, the widely fluctuating proportions of chemical components between races—still forever basil—it makes little difference, the polymorphism and extreme olfactive and chemical heterogeneity within populations—still forever basil—it makes little difference, that patterns of variation contort and shift and transpose in space and time among units of basil plants—still forever basil.

"The secret formulas of the scientist."

There are tarragon-like and thyme-like and anise-like and cinnamon-like and lemon-like strains of basil, methyl chavicol-rich and eugenol-rich and linalol-rich and camphor-rich and methyl cinnamate-rich forms of basil, French Comorian Indian Thailandian Zanzibarian Nepalese Bulgarian Haitian Egyptian Russian Pakistani Spanish Vietnamese Moroccan Guatemalan Malagasy and North African types of basil, wild and cultivated field populations of basil, basil plants distilled when dry and others when fresh (better).

"The master keys of the artist."

There are basil extracts used to produce brandies, incense and liniments, clove oils and food flavors, vanilla tinctures and aromatic nerve tonics, basil oils employed diversely to quell menstrual cramps or palliate athralgia, ease allergic rhinitis or subdue gastric upset, calm local inflammation or provoke blood flow when used as a rubefacient, basil for fever rabies nausea tumor ringworm coughing snakebite malaria ... and perfume.

"The guiding principles of the cleric."

Yet there is no good way to chart any of this? no possibility to superimpose a template and concisely classify, no manner to match morphotype to chromotype to ecotype to chemotype, no method to neatly correlate chemistry with weather with morphology with geography with phylogeny with cultural applications with biological activity with cultivation and production methods—linkages are aplenty yet inconsistent, confounding even.

"Everyone craves the code."

So how shall we best make out the basis of basil? the negotiation between variousness and unity, the enigmatic dance of accommodation that takes place within the world of this thing, this entity … basil. The biotic scenario we face could perhaps be appreciated with the help of an encapsulating axiom:

"Different articles and affairs of Life, in different ways diverge and unite, sounds right?"

All the same, with respect to our appraisal of basil, we endeavor to become better at navigating the maze of variation we find among this balkanized constellation of plants, so very assorted yet still curiously cohering together … as basil, and better at how to identify and take measure of the basis of deviation and integrity of aesthetic expression (wish us good luck, and let us know should you strike upon a good cipher).

"Presenting itself right before our eyes, it should be plain to recognize."

Saffron initiates the ritual of beholding, sending scentful samples for passing along the chain of panel members present, "The sample from France (*herbe royal*) serves a verdant impression of fresh-cut leaves in a cool breeze teeming with busy bees—I'd say, a display of, say, something like hay soaking in a cordial, like in an achingly mellifluous pastis—or rather, a bracing herbaceous tonic or digestif, only faintly sweet—try the holy basil, it effluviates layers like tides of clovey tones—and this one, a molecular benediction from Egypt, a vaporish spice box—next is what, a Mexican basil? which is surprisingly woodsy?—the soothing effect is like a fragrant dream of cream of fennel soup—"

"We know that it will materialize, when we meet with it in whichever guise."

"...this coarser *Reunion* type goes by estragole, synonymous with methyl chavicol which provides anisic liquorice tonality—the Thailand type could be mistaken for melissa? or combava petitgrain? a citrus twist? lemon-kissed? (a hesperidic tryst?)—a turn following is themed upon properties of peppery allspice, then warm tea, then hot earth—notice the shade of styrofoam?—huh?—this next aeolian has a chilly minty headnote like a cineolic speedboat, makes sense?—most of these basils are blowy and flowy and airy and *fresco*—the joint olfactive manifesto seems to emanate from pesto."

So what shall we extract from this exercise? What understanding can be distilled? insight concentrated? meaning condensed? lesson spun out and boiled down? That the observed display of discrepancy is the language of natural variety which is actually the language of Earthly vitality, being the language of biotic disparity being the state of organic irregularity being biological reality?

"To simplify is to falsify, and yet not to simplify is to remain incoherent," Saffron recites from her journal of clippings on evolution.

Let's say, that Life is for us an ever-changing dynamic story of live interest ... on the grounds that we rarely find any sort of hard and constant definitional breaks, only shifting transitional degrees resting on elusive specificities, fluxing and fluid variations resting on passing particularities ... leading us finally to concede to make peace with the unfathomableness of Creation.

"For those taking notes, it is with intention that we cap the letter C in Creation."

Still we wonder ... whereas the multitude of basil plants are integrated in myriad ecologies of Life involving billions of bits of information assembled during inconceivable numbers of evolutionary events, nonetheless the wealth of different forms appears to convey variations of a common message. What is that message?

"A single concept, a distinct contour, a basic shape ... let's say, Goethe's *Grundgestalt*?"

What makes basil always basil always basil? Some say there is cohesion due to delimited gene transfer, others play up a more opaque interplay of divergence and likeness, emergent consolidating and separating qualities of organic Life identified only with great difficulty, emphasizing that every alive being has some kind of interior essence that beanbag genetic programs have difficulty accounting for.

"An archetypal form, an ideal development, an essential process ... let's say, Goethe's *Urphänomen*?"

Supposing commonality involves organization rather than composition? that the term *basil* does not denote any given well-balanced conformation, not any given harmonious structure or stable state, but instead something more like a strategy for living, a loose plan, a broad approach, like a proven biological institution, like an evolutionary foundation developed among efflorescing Life in order to preserve certain subtle ways to flourish in the World? Along these lines, we'd view Nature as comprising representatives or graduates of such programs ... plants and perfumes.

"Basil is an element of the husk, while this inquiry bears on the core of Creation?"

Let's put it this way—inasmuch as these aromatic agents of autotrophic Life demonstrate the play of chance and necessity, randomness is plenty evident, but in the case of basil, what's the common necessity?

"A unifying principle? a primal phenomenon? an inherent lawfulness?"

Put another way (I recall a quote but can't place the source)— insofar as art expresses that which is restrained, the essence of every picture is the frame. So then, for plants that we label as basil, plants distinguished by whatever those virtues are that are faithful to the label basil ... what constitutes the frame? (not a trick question).

Perfumes of Amassment

"Fuming over fumes again?" Saffron says.

There's a connection between the cache of perfumes stored at the *perfumería* and those noxious nocturnal vapors emanating from the area of town inhabited by brickmakers.

"Granted, we are in the business of sending up flares to reveal pernicious stealth operations."

So first, understand, *narcotraficantes* are burdened with mountains of paper dollar money in the United States, which they'd like to convert into mountains of paper peso money in Mexico. But it's not so easy as before to pay off *aduanas* officials and pass across the border with cash-stuffed suitcases.

"This is troubling to the banksters of the smuggling gangsters."

So the narcos' favored techniques have been one or another variation of trade-based money laundering, by which dollars aren't smuggled, but placed instead toward the acquisition of goods for import to Mexico. The purchased commodities then serve as currency, transported unobtrusively over the crossing.

"Sneakers electronics cigarettes computers and liquors, small appliances and auto parts and—"

And ... perfumes are especially fancied by narcos as currency, owing to their inertness and good value, and because the suspicions of customs agents aren't raised since the valuation of such cultural curiosities has always appeared arbitrary. Large shipments thus rarely invite scrutiny, even when they're greatly undervalued on paper.

"Have you heard that two children were just found dead nearby? stuffed into a cardboard box. The *Procuraduría* ruled death by accident."

Black market *cambistas* (dollar-peso exchangers) are enlisted to obscure money trails, making the program complicated, hard to audit by design. Their agents in the United States accept duffel bags of dollars to initiate the brokerage, and their people in Mexico facilitate this side of the transactions, deduct their commissions, and pay out the (truckloads of) paper pesos due the *narcotraficantes*.

"The *Ministerio Público* considered the possibility that the kids were playing and suffocated. It sounds suspicious, sure, but we don't really know."

Certain drug traffickers have already been busted for implementing such an illicit scheme, inspiring the news media to broadcast the catchy headline: *the stench of dirty money is masked with the scent of perfume.*

"Those mixed up with the *perfumería* across the way, they're not really in the perfume business (you knew that). Earlier at the *tiendita* I met someone from over there. We shared a three-peso *Camello* smoke, and got to talking..."

Because there is always so much money to launder, the *cambistas* are helpless but to import surplus perfume. So I suspect that your friends are cleaning up, trying to unload the surfeit, to do something with the leftovers. And their shop also functions as a front company.

"They work a scheme to dispose of the chemical waste by the choking fires of the *pobres ladrilleros*."

In many Mexico cities there are weekly *tianguis*, sprawling markets where anomalous vendors may be selling new watches and sunglasses, jewelry and perfumes at deep discounts. We've always assumed that much of that merchandise is stolen, but now we might consider otherwise, that the goods are perhaps residue of a money-laundering operation.

"Have you peaked behind the *perfumería* front counter? Just behind the packing case of Tom Ford *Black Orchid* is a pile of bulletproof vests."

The security paraphernalia is stacked near a box of Kenneth Cole *Mankind,* which is promoted as a fragrance for the modern stand-up guy.

Perfumes of Distinction

Moses, according to the Book of Exodus, was instructed by God (appearing partial to myrrh) on how to make incense?

"But ask now the beasts and they shall teach thee, and the fowls of the air, and they shall tell thee—" Saffron is now quoting from Job?

No, it's wrong to suggest I'm a partisan for fragrant art, at least I haven't been so from the beginning. I advocate on behalf of aromatics because it's where I've arrived after decades of searching, and now, yes, I'm like a drumbeating exponent, because I can't find another to closely rival plant perfume as a currency of vital wisdom.

"Or speak to the Earth and it shall teach thee—"

Music is the language of love, dwelling in the realm of romance, justly celebrated as first citizen of that ethereal domain, while barely rooted, as if by tenuous superficial rhizomes, in the world of matter and motion. Whereas you can listen to sounds, you won't see them, or touch them, as this affecting acoustic medium is made up of pressure waves, which have no mass.

"Nor are such transmissions strongly linked to Life. Bear in mind that the reverberating tones of abiotic ocean waves and atmospheric winds are arguably just as compelling as those emanating from living coyotes and crickets."

The aesthetic analysis of music is like an exercise in chasing elusory shadows of butterflies, in that it requires nimble cognitive stretching and reaching, what with so much more fancy to account for than form to grasp.

"And the fishes of the sea shall declare unto thee—"

No, no way am I biased against music. Not a chance will I be pitted against this means of expression that I hold so dear. Yet still, the resonant medium doesn't much reconcile or bridge or traverse fields of knowing, rather it holds permanent residence in the heart and rarely ventures a visit elsewhere.

"And music is not in the business of Earthly endorsements."

When I'm asked why the likes of so many fascists and sadists and other such sociopaths love music? as much as anyone? I explain that melodies and rhythms don't take a stand, that in cases of concrete conflicts, music sides with no cause over another, advocating only for itself.

"That is, vibrational waves of music waver."

The nature of this art form is so abstract that musicians, as a rule rarely broken, compose with an ear toward tangible structure, melodic and harmonic and rhythmic—as say, a memorable motif, a percussive pattern, repeating series of pitches, redundant combinations of tones, anything grounded, of substance to lend familiarity, to grab onto, to access.

"Schoenberg symphonies were known to incite abusive heckling."

Notwithstanding those exceptions, which are scarce and arguably gratuitous, even the most experimental of musical experiments hardly betrays the call of music for intelligibility and order.

"Seeing and agreeing that hearing, once a leading way of perceiving, is appearing to be persevering, its preceding of seeing is simply meaning that seeing is seeming to be less anteceding."

Next in order . . . is our perception of visual art, whereby our attention is directed, not to the electromagnetic energy by which an object is sensed, but to the concrete object itself, our eyes focusing upon a material thing taking up space in this physical World, a terrestrial entity that can be viewed and described, touched and held and tangibly scrutinized, its development traced and its contents inspected, as its constituting elements are overt, with properties that are outwardly apparent, with palpable substance that can be recognized and parsed, like solid meat for us thinking-bound to chew on.

"Yet again, visible artworks aren't strongly linked to Life. Bear in mind that paintings of inorganic stars and seas may be just as engaging as those of metabolizing beings like orchids and horses."

But creations from hues and shapes, on exhibit for viewing, have less potency for stirring emotions, for pulling heartstrings and shaking spirits. They are weighted down in a sense, so that artists are less beckoned to create visuals with structured or ordered patterns, but rather, are routinely seduced by the airiness of abstraction.

"Try this—hike a temperate rainforest stocked with millions of plants and fungi and microorganisms—you'll notice that, no matter which way you look, the color green predominates. Where is all the expectable visual signaling?"

And so, gessoed canvases rubbed over by pigmented oils seem to invite extravagantly imaginative art criticism, while chin-rubbing and head-scratching loquaciousness by beholders at art gallery receptions is, can we say, cliché?—it goes with the show, not so?

"And again, just like music, the medium is inherently impartial, bearing no intrinsic calls to action, thereby leaving the door wide open for the ardent patronage by whatever immoral actor, whatever gangster or bankster or other such crooked character who loves pictorial art as much as the next malefactor."

(Artists working in the different media, taken together, appear to triangulate between counterpoising poles, between the sensible and conceptual, the defined and rarified, pulling away from the extremities of Earthliness and dreaminess, where subjects are explicit or in spirit, to find some middle position.)

But perfume? An emissive fragrant agent can burn a hole in your skin and your soul both—how is that to reconcile outer and inner realities? to patch together that which is below with that above?

"Nature has neither core nor skin, she's both at once outside and in," this I recognize as Goethe.

Plant perfumes command center stage in our physical domain yet also unseal the hidden other, spanning that gap that is wider than the sky. Volatile oils are unmistakably present, impactful infochemicals with measurable mass, yet are also elusive, serving as substantive food for our forebrain thinking while at the same time instigating upon us the subtle stuff, the unmediated effects, taking a bypass route around the neencephalic thalamus and rushing head-on into the evolutionarily ancient paleocephalic limbic-system brain and endocrine glands, the seats of feelings and fancies and reminiscences ... and mystery.

"Sound hasn't any legs to stand on. Color is on a three-legged dinner tray. Fragrance is at once to Nature tethered, while floating unfettered."

What other currency of information can rival this enigmatic behavior? to demand attention concurrently in the magisteria of chemists and priests? to be associated both with moral decay and devotional sacrament? condemned as hedonistic excess while consecrated as holy revelation? in which fragrant intoxicants are outlawed while aromatic demonifuges guarded? erotic unguents scorned while incense for religious rituals sanctified?

"Perfume principles incarnate materialized alongside the ideated etherealized."

I trust our assertions are finally shaking through. Next, we'll discuss that close alignment and mighty affiliation with Life, that has changed my life, to provoke on behalf of Life, the phenomenon of Life.

"In whose hand is the soul of every living thing, and the breath of all mankind."

Perfumes of Homology
(Catmint)

It's not to chatter in the manner of a palaver when we dutifully gather to take up the matter of Life.

"Evidently, whenever a deliberate search is made, communication by the agency of perfume is identified as predominating," Saffron greets our guests.

Found in volatile secretions of bees ants beetles butterflies mammals and many others, plant perfumes constitute a deeply rooted organic messaging medium employed by animals across divergent lines of descent.

"Found in fragrant vapors emanating from foliage fruits barks roots seeds stems spores and flowers, animal scents constitute a deeply rooted organic messaging medium employed by plants across divergent lines of descent?"

Of course, our attention is usually drawn to colors and sounds of birds and large vertebrates, whose sensory physiology more resembles our own.

"Most people are unaware that biological interactivity by means of perfume is as old as Creation itself."

Most are unacquainted with natural history, and how that inquiry bears on the relevancy of biochemistry, in that the taxonomic distribution of chemical communication spans the phylogenetic gamut of Life. For a quick and easy survey ... we now join in the evolutionary pageant, picking up with the green alga *Volvox* and protozoan *Paramecium* which put proteinaceous chemicals to use in order to activate the production of sperm, or alternatively to recognize mates, then we continue on, with female brown algae which employ specialized gynogamones to function in the attraction of their male gametic counterparts, then the female *Allomyces* water mold which invites the approach of sperm by sending out the oxygenated sesquiterpene sirenin, then the fungus *Mucor* which also puts gamones to work with the objective of influencing male gametes to draw near, then slime molds which employ a chemotactic agent to set an aggregating locomotion in motion, then ferns which emit perfumes for inducing gametophytes to develop antheridia, then earthworms which issue alarm pheromones that send conspecifics wriggling away—

"Take a breath, Salonnier."

...then aquatic snails which sound polypeptide alarms, then crabs and many spiders which commission chemical compounds to avail in attracting females, then barnacles and rotifers which project select perfumes for pointed effects, then the list goes on, eventually arriving at the huge class of entomic three-segmented arthropods that comprise three-quarters of all known animals ...yes, insects, which are so famously associated with practices of exuding metabolic agents in the service of recognition and alarms and trails and repellence and disruption and poisoning and excitation and aggregation and camouflaging and dispersal and sex, molecular messaging both common and widespread, and then also, by all means, fish and amphibians and reptiles and mammals, which also bear a share of such fare, as vertebrates administer a wide variety of fragrant courtship and territorial signaling systems.

"The transmission of infochemicals appears to characterize every limb and branch and twig of biological descent borne on the great arborescent shrub of Life."

"It asserts a quality that's especially earthy—that is, soily—it is oily—which is synonymous with oleaginous—which is analogous to cannabis—it's herby in reality—woody actually—which is vernacularly ligneous—seedy really—this sample's a handful," the salonists have begun salonizing.

First flight this evening ... catnip? no way. Are you thinking of calamintha? often taken for catmint, plants of which release to the air, via glandular hairs, a perfume that is a great deal easier on the nares.

"As to catnip (*cataire citronnée*) ... the headnotes are heady, the forwardmost most blameworthy, and inasmuch as the principal aspects are pungently expressed, counting an explicitly sweet-toned interpretation of the broad association we think of as sweetness, more than anything, there is an herbal evocation, an intense fuming impression of herbaceousness."

The primary bioactive constituent, nepetalactone, also carries out duties as a defense semiochemical, secreted by coconut-stick insects and aphids, and from the abdominal glands of rove beetles.

"The blanket character exhibits a rough texture and is harsh-leaning, yet still there's a slight minty principle that isn't displeasing, a tea and clary-like feature that suits me—the fronting compounds are aggressive, in this case they make an effusive headspace, on that we agree?—much as the backnotes don't diffuse as much, and the spicy underbedding is dull as such, in context the full bouquet seems almost a refined touch."

Isomeric nepetalactone, considered an opioid analgesic, is dispatched along with other metabolic messengers of catnip perfume, often in league with a consorting compound, beta-caryophyllene.

"Nepetalactone is also used by hunters to lure bobcats and mountain lions, so that they can take pleasure to shoot them ... and then watch them suffer and die."

The next oil has a citrusy composition, presently being passed among percipients, a selection representative of the distinct catnip variety, citriodora.

"Whereas this sample emerges again as leafy, it comes on greener and less obtrusive as it parades a floating hesperidate radiance that is, we find, largely undermined by a cresylic note— the milder drydown is hay-like and lemony with a tailing understated geranium statement."

There is a certain field of endeavor, a contrived line of study—so-called aromachology—that was conceived by Perfume Industry functionaries with a view to promote the range of aromatic oil activities. However, the human responses they register are confined, bear in mind, to those of the mind, which is how aromachology is defined, limited to effects upon the psyche, effects that involve cognitive and emotional function, in other words, effects on the spirit, the delineation is explicit. And also keep in mind that the powerful perfumery crime family is panic-threatened by incontrovertible notions championed by *aromathérapie* adherents concerning wide-ranging biological responses to plant extracts.

"And cats who salivate and do backward flips upon exposure to catnip?"

At present, perfumes of commerce are officially considered cosmetics. And we suspect that the designation *aromachology* was actually a brainchild of scheming lawyers, on behalf of executives and shareholders, number crunchers and actuaries, all worried about financial liabilities and frightened of regulatory implications were such mass perfumes ever to be taken for drugs.

"The crafty chemical venturers invoke psychology to account for the feline folly?"

The volatile principle nepetalactone is primarily what triggers the unhinged behavior. And while the psychoactive vapors might reveal the purpose of their mission at the site of olfactory epithelium, there is no mistaking that the basis of the inebriation is physiological.

"Cats under the influence of perfume."

Over five hundred documented scientific studies establish how essential oils exert measurable actions upon our organs, our blood and lymphatic fluids, our bones and connective tissue. All the same, Perfume Industry rebuttals are delivered as spreadsheet arguments, cynical slogans, gift certificates, twisted smiles, and letters from attorneys.

"The partisans and pawns, apostles and addicts, supporters and *sicarios*."

Perfumes of Association

"Some of you have asked about the thousands of scintillation vials that make up our reference library."

This next phase of orientation will acquaint you with lab practices and techniques, record keeping and label making, diluting and pipetting procedures, working with scales, and calculating formulas.

"You'll learn of our routines, what we do behind the scenes, our weighty ways and measured means: we generate accords—we combine volatiles in keeping with themes—we go about accord building—we're filling our time by fulfilling our charge to create accords," Saffron presides over today's class.

We can't overemphasize the role for this manner of aromatic improvisation, the construction of character-forming building blocks, vehicles for juxtapositional study and stepping stones to advanced composition (accords are sometimes confused with bases, which constitute only a subset).

"We are scheduled to embrace a most elegant case of emergence in action, for the process will materialize before us by the marriage of perfume principles."

Accords may comprise molecular bridges or dances of disassociation, may be spartan or elaborate or stratified or integrated or horizontal or vertical, may be formed of elements complementary or contrasting or reinforcing or cohering or transforming or bolstering, may serve in furtherance of harmony or tension or balance or distinctness or coalescence or surprise.

"Shall we then? ready for the show? get set, go—a courtship between osmanthus and rose otto, a promising combo? to empower orange flower try melilot, to manifest an alchemical rendering of depth and longevity, saffron with black pepper and not too much (or it's oily) boronia, orris root embellished by the slightest trace (or it's vomitous) of green cognac, we suggest a test tying expressed zest of lime to our best plai, and thyme anyone? Peru balsam plus ylang makes an odorful coordination that connotes carnation, enhanced and richened by clove bud, or Roman chamomile to impart herbal notes, tweaked and boosted by cinnamon bark, widened and exalted by a floralizer, you choose…"

Forgive this tangent, but I have an image affixed in my mind—of a hardworking mom and dad in springtime 1943 Poland, who are protective of their children, who worry about the future, hoping that they lead worthy lives, and each day observe abundant pale smoke rise and fan out from a nearby death camp, the destination of railcars that transport communists and gypsies, homosexuals and Jews.

"Heavy implicitness is summoned by our exercises in explicitness."

The clouds of silvery ash and plumes of incineration products move in patterns depending on the direction of local winds, turning to light dust that falls all around and leaves a thin draping film on the organic vegetables and herbs in their garden. Every few days they brush with feathers this cinereous powder from the plants, beets carrots chard lettuce and asparagus, onions interplanted with cole crops to ward off cabbage butterflies, each planting according to phases of the moon.

"Continuing: add musty methyl anthranilate at the fusty hand of mandarin to modify the tonality of orange oil? build it up with bergamot for lingering dulcification? supplement with savory to give a lively phenolic aspect, tobacco with tuberose, mix in vanilla oleoresin, perhaps guaiacwood, eucalyptus with lemongrass, oak moss or alternatively davana into lavender to experiment with classic chypre and *fougère* compositions, altered and fixed by clary sage, sweetened by labdanum resinoid, birch tar for smokiness, or cypress to bestow a coniferous element, to lead in the direction of evergreen woodlands..."

Whereas adherents in molecular gastronomy pursue similar sorts of pairings, they are especially partial to chemical bridges. For instance, they suppose methyl hexanoate will connect oysters with kiwi fruit? So we should rather not dwell on the wide-ranging slew of other such experimental matches of modernist cuisine: say, like sage and peanuts? blue cheese and pineapple? chocolate and caraway? mint and mustard, banana and parsley, asparagus and violet, strawberry and coriander, apple and lavender, coffee and capers?

"The designation *molecular* is misleading since those culinary investigators aren't compounding foods with discrete molecules."

Likewise, molecular mixologists aren't barkeeps formulating libations from individual chemical compounds. Rather, the scentful alcoholic drinks they're throwing together are mostly bathed with integral expressions straight from Nature, and the palette of materials they access release metabolic vapors that are ready-assembled by the enigmatic strokes of Creation.

"Each shake of the cocktail mixer is a dance in praise of biological particularity and natural diversity."

We figure, they are proud quirky partisans who affiliate with the idiosyncratic specificities of Life, connoisseurs who revel in immediate small things, who appreciate subliminal traces and fluid interfaces, who value unorthodox combinations and nuanced differences.

"Behind the bar, until four in the morning, they stand on behalf of unfolding vitality and Earthly integrity and impenetrable intricacy."

They're enlisted in the army of artisans fighting against virtuality and simulation, in special units crafting cordials that are rallying cries for improvisation against contrivance, flux against stasis, variousness against standards. Their allegiance is borne out by all the fresh ingredients that they use in the moment, of which the labile components would be long gone by the deferred time of widespread product distribution.

"Continuing: why not amend our borneol camphor tincture by the addition of spikenard? work in a trace of choya for a campfire chord? merge carrot seed with costus, spice up a rosemary herbal with hyssop and hops, blend blackcurrant with tagette, much as such a mixture wouldn't be for the faint of heart? apply lavandin to instill in patchouli an esteric essence and some cineolic buoyancy, and galbanum to confer some active olfactive verdancy, or to complement the anisic quality of basil, with tonka bean doubling as a hay tone and coumarinic fixative ... lead hedychium to champa, once conjoined their assimilation is guaranteed ... introduce agarwood to bakul, once incorporated the sensory revelation is guaranteed to be baffling ... and now, for some easy kyphi recipes..."

So, in any case, how did Nazis get all the names of European Jews? identify and catalogue and trace ancestries? locate and register and ghettoize? confiscate assets, deport, and run railroads? organize slave labor and mass murder? How could they conduct such a campaign if no computers existed?—the answer is IBM punch card machines. And the cards were customized for the concentration camps and serviced on site, in every camp.

"American heedlessness paired with German precision, what a combination."

The prisoner card codes read *Juden* number eight, *Bibelforscher* number two, referring to Jehovah's Witnesses, *Rotspanier* number six, referring to communists from Spain, *homosexueller* number three, and so on.

"American promiscuity paired with German perfectionism, what an accord."

"Continuing: next, consider chancing a fine melding in which jasmine sambac is swayed by an extract of rose de Mai in order to establish a certain proportionality of florality meaning a distinct floral focus and then consider also a helping of helichrysum to radiate honey-like notes as well as a share of geranium to augment the flowery veneer and maybe a serving of celery seed for perky warmth and lastly perhaps a last drop of sandalwood as a blender or at least as a stabilizer so the working accord will be lasting."

Good start.

Perfumes of Incorporation

"We're threatened by the knowledge that death is coming, panicked by what we know, not acceding to how life ends, not conceding to how it goes, so we set about with methods of evasion, determined to somehow change the equation."

Umm, let's see, a sculpture, a painting, a poem, an engraving, a symphonic score, and lots more, but perfume? I don't think so.

"We blame and scream, complain and scheme, any charade in order to evade, any delaying to keep from paying ... Nature's debt."

Lofty chemical artworks of matchless animation can't be fixed in time, can't make a permanent record. And a state of ephemerality is an inherent handicap for an art form (insert here a nod to street-artist Banksy). With perfume, the very act of beholding an aromatic dispatch involves its dissolution or occasional sublimation.

"The vapors emanate and disseminate, diffuse and dissipate."

Molecule after molecule breaks off from an atomic lattice in order to entice and beseech, to solicit and display, elicit and sway. Thus we speak of direct experience: segments of a fragrant formulation peel away in order to score points with you, slough off from their origins for the benefit (and occasional penalty) of your reception, for your welcoming perception (and occasional rejection).

"Not pleased with how it goes, not accepting of how it's scheduled to end, we try to move beyond Life, to upset the balance somehow, to reorder our experience of Nature, to welcome the onset of virtual reality, to establish residence in a world where Earthly agency depreciates and abstract activity appreciates."

Perhaps you'd rather that a recipe for perfume serve as does a recipe for music (a musical score)? But fragrant principles never come to a standstill—*elles sont dynamiques*. Whereas the b-flat in Wagner's Sonata is sure to remain so, the cedar element in Sheldrake's *Féminité du Bois* will never rest—the lavender principle in Kurkdjian's *Le Male* will never stop moving—the basil component in Roudnitzka's *Diorella* will never stay put—at least, not if the constituents exhibit attributes of vitality.

"Sorry to inform you ... that there is nothing alive in such mainstream fragrances as you reference."

Because, see, commercial perfumes are inert, just as much as the goggles and gloves of the compounding chemist. There is nothing vital in the iconic *eau de toilette* by Edmond Roudnitzka, the accoladed father of the molecule-twiddling mass practice called modern perfumery.

"We record and fix artworks in sound and color, no problem, but snapshots of tirelessly fluxing scented surprises?—no, don't think so."

Because, see, inasmuch as the phenomenon of living denotes continuous temporality and perpetual change, the fact that contemporary perfumes are relatively invariant and fixed bears on the matter of their aliveness, and whether they reflect any life or even lifelikeness. In any case, Sheldrake and Kurkdjian and

Roudnitzka would rather not be bothered with such a query, and neither would their fraternal and idealogical allies, all those biophobic barons and alpha-heroic magi of cosmological musing and Nature abusing.

"*L'chaim l'chaim* to life," Saffron appears to have memorized Hebrew lines from the stage musical.

Because, see, any given snapshot of emissive art that you experience olfactively—if it's alive, in the way that volatile expressions of Nature are alive—is different from the snapshot available to others. But what is the precise difference? how would we measure? in what units? with what instruments?—there's no way—poetic, no? to experience the very features of the living, woven together to give form to the idea.

"Idea?"

The unthinkable idea.

"Of Life?"

Of the epic unqualifiable anomalous story.

"It has a way of confusing us, blessing us and bruising us, *l'chaim l'chaim* to life," we're treated to a musical coda.

Perfumes of Variegation
(Geranium)

Synthetic lies travel around the World in the time that metabolic truths put on their shoes.

"Yes, this evening, ready and waiting, are a wide range of geranium expressions for presentation after just a minute's break," Saffron announces.

Oh, then first, briefly (really), while we wait, I'll relate, that during the late nineteenth century, with the state of organic chemistry changing, and the fate of plant perfumes waning, as the rate of falsification was gaining, there were still occasional runs scored (yay) by the home team (hooray) of Life.

"Representations of Life were hanging on for dear life."

A certain geranium provides an example: while introduced around 1880 for cultivation on the Indian Ocean island of Réunion (previously *Ile de Bourbon*) for its pleasing integral oil, subsequently the predominant chemical components (geraniol, citronellol, nerol, 2-phenylethanol, menthone) would draw the biggest share of commercial attention, familiar to brokers as products of industrial synthesis. Yet still, even today, the geranium bourbon of same provenance continues to be valued for its exemplary whole distilled oil complex of inimitably pronounced green-leafy rose alcohols and entwining earthy minty notes that exalt a fruity facet leading into an extended ambrosial rosy tailing.

"Sorry to say, but geranium oils presently are often compounded to contrived standards."

Achh, that announcement brings me down. It recalls to my mind the extensive global machinery of manipulation and control by the template for shaping states of affairs with abstract exercises of idealization. And so, genuine Nature is increasingly trumped by reproductions of Nature, perfumes pressed under the thumb of the world system of power-thought, of domination and conquest.

"Soapers motivated by marketplace savings should realize the *Pelargonium* extracts they procure are rarely those authentic of Living Nature."

We're full up to here with philosophers, who are forever frustrated by novel phenomena, reluctant denizens of the mesokosmos (of Ernst Mayr) or middle world (of Richard Dawkins) familiar to our senses, and full up to here with physicists, who say that a flower is virtually all empty space, that the universe is an idea formed of mathematics, and full up to here with mystics, who sit cross-legged to inhabit worlds everywhere and nowhere at once, we're full up to here with all of them, fixated on places smaller than molecules than electrons than atomic nuclei than quarks and bigger than stellar bodies than quasars than black holes than dark matter than the ultra-galactic and cosmic, who are fascinated by movement slower than geologic formations and faster than the speed of light, and full up to here also with insatiable *empresarios* who similarly behave as if all materiality is temporary and all consciousness and all that we experience are ultimately streams of numbers.

"Granted, any given number that you designate, say the number eight, is never ever any different from any other number eight. Any given number that you pick, say the number six, is never ever any different from any other number six."

The love affair that has consumed humanity, with abstract symbols and methods and situation-free facts and rational systems and universal laws … benign?—tell that to the hundred thousand residents of August 6, 1945 Hiroshima, who couldn't find their faces after a B-29 bomber dropped upon them, from the skies, Edward Teller's proofs and theorems.

"In any case, sometimes broad concepts come to light in the course of looking into narrative accounts of inferred chance non-repeating interactions in Nature."

Whereas those sold on Life-loathing notions of generality to the snubbing disregard of particular rivers raptors redbuds resins and reptiles may start foregoing or holding instead or may be beheld upholding a sympathetic beholding of the ongoing flowing unfolding of living—

Saffron interrupts, "So, goodbye airy fancies in the matter of meaning? of purpose and salvation?—and hello real-World horseflies porcupines sundews mildew borages rodents garbage turpentine columbines and cabbage?"

Right, goodbye blank canvases in painting and toneless decompositions in music—and hello blossoms bearing pollen and melons with their seeds yielding weeds and specific breeds of peppers and capers and boundary layers of aromatic vapors.

"So, goodbye unlimited frontiers and perfect or at least ideal solutions to pressing human problems? goodbye suggestions of a new reality for humanity?—and hello randomness of natural happenings? hello designless diversification and haphazard transmogrification? hello mosaic evolution that's glacially slow, directionless and conditional and opportunistic?

Right, goodbye quantum field theory, Pauli exclusion and Heisenberg uncertainty principles, goodbye geometric figures, algorithms and academic constructs of space and time, mass and motion, goodbye whimsical sentiments of human preeminence and eventual transcendence—and hello animal curiosity and actual novelty, hello explicit organic efflorescence and distinct biological remaking and self-renewal, hello esthetic delight and poetic feeling, running and dancing and resting, and just being.

"Goodbye again, now to begin—this round leading, rounding the table, is an interesting material of ethanolic extraction from India."

The whole fresh herb is first subject to petroleum ether, then mixed with alcohol, which is subsequently removed under vacuum. The resulting oil is powerfully rosaceous, with a central chord underscored by certain lemon and gingergrass notes that attempt to distinguish themselves, to sway the bouquet. And more, a sneaky pitched whisper of something cheesy—

"The sour reekiness is owing to a hydrolytic transaction in which butyric acid has gotten the better of a butyrate ester."

Oh no, here it comes, one of those headaches, the kind induced by convoluting debates over plant taxonomy and nomenclature, which pertains to geranium in that hundreds of species have been identified in South Africa, the *Pelargonium* center of diversification, especially the southwestern Cape region of winter rainfall, whence vegetative cuttings were exported in the late seventeenth century to Kew and other botanical institutes in Europe to be

THE PERFUME OF LIFE · BOOK ONE

cross-pollinated (being that the displaced plants were so prone, absent geographic barriers of home, isolating features of their native range), thereupon yielding new hybrids and varieties and cultivars, and then re-exported, especially to French colonies, where a proliferation of commercial taxa were introduced, most of which were exuberantly scented shrubs, thereby inciting confusion over proper names and derivations.

"By virtue of the fragrant elicitations they let off, emissions that mimic the vaporous calling cards of assorted herbs and resins, spices and fruits—lemon pineapple mint ginger cinnamon frankincense nutmeg strawberry—such plants were bestowed names such as attar of roses, lemon meringue, and apple mint."

The biggest headache, however, comes on with questions involving the prized bourbon type, the *rosé* cultivar, interchangeably referred to as rose geranium, *géranium rosat*. People in the business readily assert their proprietary ideas about its origins and specifications as if they are collaborating on a work of fiction? And confusion around the name is exploited by traders, or so-called bulkers, who can't help but distribute reconstituted forgeries of place and substance. The lab-made molecule diphenyl oxide, for instance, is applied to doctor exports of rose geranium from the Orient.

"The Réunion product is most reputable, anyone interested?"

Portugal Spain Italy Cuba El Salvador Japan Haiti Israel and some African nations have developed operations without much success except for some Congo distillates which are exceedingly sweet though less mentholic than the more established Malagasy renderings which send out a fast-evaporating sulphide trace and give off a fading fresh-fizzy effusion—

"Not so fast, and it's all right to gasp, Salonnier, for air."

…but then again which lack the tobacco-woody underpinning of the Egyptian selections which issue in turn volatiles less herby than those more earthy of the Moroccan oils which also resemble yet are more penetrating than the Russian at the same time that the French are characteristically fine-rosy while the Indian are less so and harsher with lemon-peppery references these being uncharacteristic of the Chinese which are most minty of all moreover with soapy accents lingering.

"Fronting this next flushing sample I notice an unusual tweak of a plastic-metallic attribute, can that be right? in the forwardly phenolic sense?—the toned-down citrus tones come on curiously, almost deep-set, not really like top-notes, rather they seem soft-pedaled as if held and settled among deep-going principles of a radiant heart? and shaping that fraction is a commanding traction of rose-shaded floweriness—also something acutely evocative is reflected, lavender lip balm or motel bar soap? Thai soup with lemongrass? violet leaf or linden blossom or sweet alyssum?"

Some ascribe the can't-place-the-name syndrome, that tip-of-the-tongue trouble to your immediate perception by the right brain hemisphere, succeeded by name recognition that (sometimes stalls as it) hinges on left hemisphere activity.

"The real-live really alive essential oil, not the cynical knock-off, is a medicine-chest imperative for the hemostatic activity of a few drops on a cotton ball wrapped over a bleeding wound for a day, after which you'll notice good tissue repair."

Now, this next is a test, of your olfactory percipience:

"Much as a given geranium oil consists of many dozens of intermingling molecular constituents, it nevertheless releases an integrated cloud of volatiles recognized by most (mmm, unmistakable) as a unique aromatic entity with a memorable odorful identity, more so even than any of the individual components beheld severally, any of the metabolites experienced on their own, removed from the context of the whole plant perfume."

That is, geranium the undivided and undiminished combinative conglomerate chemical expression with the confounding and inconsistent profile is more reliably identifiable than any of the single invariant compounds contained. Explain that?

Perfumes of Reverberation
(Petroleum)

We continue now to chronicle past events. This following section might prompt a recollection, it might spark a memory trace cached from the past, but whether this takes place or not, whichever, please abide the endeavor, and we'll reward your patience in some measure.

"Life, now to be laid out upon the sacrificial altar."

1820—An American chemist, Alexander Garden, working in Britain with a certain John Kidd, describes white crystals that form upon the pyrolysis (decomposition by heating) of coal tar, calling it naphthalene, a finding succeeded a few years later by Michael Faraday's working out the chemical formula ($C_{10}H_8$) of this mothball-scented substance, and some decades later by Emil Erlenmeyer's revealing the structure to be straightforwardly a couple of fused benzene rings.

"It should be plain to recognize, the reason that we emphasize—"

Soon afterwards, another crystalline chemical you may recognize, caffeine, is first isolated from coffee beans by a chemist in Germany, yet Friedrich Runge will apply much of his career to a program of deriving compounds from coal tar.

"It should be plain to recognize, chemical innovation is on the rise."

1824—And another German chemist, while busy isolating a variety of substances (stamp his name into your neuronal tissue), Friedrich Wöhler (that is, into a memory bank for later retrieval) stumbles upon a synthesis that may portend the coming revolution in organic chemistry ... he prepares oxalic acid—by all accounts an organic compound found in living organisms (responsible for that sour taste of sorrel or rhubarb leaves)—from cyanogen, an inorganic and wickedly toxic (cyanide) gas. Some declare this to be the first ever fabrication of a material that's biological from a substance that's inert.

"Some ring the liberty bell to proclaim freedom, to announce that humanity is free from the impenetrable complexity and unfathomable immensity of the wild open realm of Living Nature."

1825—That fellow Faraday is still busy burning hydrocarbons to make new discoveries of the residues. This time it's an odorous liquid remaining upon the combustion of illuminating gas derived from whale oil. Later, we'll be calling this consequential compound ... benzene.

"They ring the bell to proclaim freedom, to announce that mankind is free from the idiosyncratic specificities and fluid intricacies of Creation in process."

Am I losing my audience? to the sounds of science? Shall I provide a sixty-second primer? Here goes—the most compressed course ever in organic chemistry...

"Life, on schedule, to be sacrificed to power."

It's a sprawling subject, and would be a daunting project, to become well versed in the chemistry of biotic Nature, but you'll be well on your way if you just keep in mind that ... that all Life is held together by carbon atoms, as they are uniquely and elegantly suited to serve as elemental building blocks of Nature, and involved in innumerable kinds of molecules, often in alliance with hydrogen atoms, the two together forming hydrocarbons—sound familiar?

"Domination gains, Life drains."

These basic organic compounds are found prominently under the Earth's surface as deposits of fossil fuels, fossilized biomass, having originated from decomposed biological matter that became subject to the crockpot of geologic formations and geologic time. These C and H atoms en masse, densely compressed together and heated, are prone to develop into large chain and ring-like structures by chemical bonding, hence the abundant formation of complex hydrocarbon cocktails known to us as crude oil or petroleum and natural gas and coal.

"Petrochemicals, feedstocks for the production of a chemical bounty upon the spree of industrialism and all-around ravaging of the Natural World in store."

Petroleum is that dark soupy speculators' prize formed of prehistoric zooplankton and algae, coal the more compact combustible rocks made of ancient terrestrial plants, natural gas the separating lighter fractions formed at relatively great depths under the Earth's crust and harvested mostly from oil or gas fields. Yet all these big-time fuels and solvents are multiplex mixtures, refined variously by fractional distillation operations to yield kerosene and gasoline and cooking gas and paraffin and naphthas and lubricating oils.

"Our capacity to control inflates, Life abates."

As to coal tar, it's a thick blackish sludge, scented of naphthalene, produced by the destructive distillation or carbonization of coal.

"The old-time medication is an affirmation of old times," Saffron mimes her approval, "topical coal tar treatments are still to be found knocking around the marketplace."

As to naphthas, they are lighter liquid hydrocarbon fractions that are considerably volatile. Those of petroleum are raw materials to yield a good number of industrial derivatives.

"Manipulation gains, Life wanes."

All this is to lead up to our identification of a class of naphthas particularly odorful and powerfully dissolving, namely those from coal tar. These crude resources comprise major petrochemicals such as benzene, toluene, xylene, cresol, phenol, naphthalene, and others, important starting points for the synthesis of dyes drugs explosives preservatives and paints and ... perfumes.

"By *artificial* we mean made by men, and occasionally women who behave like men."

Along with turpentine from trees, coal-tar naphthas are primary feedstocks for the production of fragrant, mostly terpenoid, molecules for subsequent assembling into modern perfumes of commerce—

... by which we mean those aggressive agents of flagrant statements of disengagement, those diffusive runny batteries of abusive synthetic semaphores of scent.

"*Eternity* by Calvin Klein makes a rhyme with assembly line and dollar sign."

Finally (how am I on time? to address a lexical misconception?) ... it is owing to the historic appellation that coal tar derivatives are today classified as *aromatic*. Yes, they tend to be more redolent than their aliphatic or chain-like hydrocarbon counterparts, nevertheless they're distinguished not by odor but by molecular structure—the incorporation of six carbon atoms in a (benzene) ring with three double bonds—the geometry causes electrons to behave differently, as they become delocalized, more spread around, and the molecules are thus less reactive. So the term *aromaticity* denotes a chemical behavior of comparatively low reactivity.

"Not much of an organic chemistry primer and not even close to sixty seconds."

So now, this excursus brings us back to the point of diversion from our timeline, to Faraday's 1825 research analyzing whale-oil residues and his discovery of ... benzene, the first in a homologous series of aromatic hydrocarbons that play heavily in the commodification and counterfeiting of Nature.

"But we have scheduled soon, perhaps the most seminal event for us to cover..."

Perfumes of Acknowledgment

"I'm having the time of my life."

Vivisectionists maim or murder, in the United States alone, over ten thousand animals each hour. And that's not counting the mice and birds tortured or killed, since those numbers are too great to tally.

"You're the life of the party."

No, I'm not sorry, and I won't apologize for my insistent repeating that biological Life, along with expressions of life, expressions that reflect life, that is, reflect the distinguishing nature of Life, they are today fully under siege.

"So where have you been all my life?"

Salonists, this is not to bring you down, but you should assign the following vernacular terms to memory: *Entambados* are bodies of murder victims placed in oil drums that are then filled with cement. *Encobijados* are bodies wrapped in rugs or blankets and tied up for disposal. *Encajuelados* are bodies stuffed into trunks of cars. *Encintados* are victims bound and blindfolded with tape.

"Jumping up first from the scent blotter bearing a sample of our sample, from a distillation of parsley herb, setting the emanation in motion, ahead of the collective embodiment to follow, are scattered zestful leafy principles, camphorous and thymol-like, whereas the main complexion is generously bracing and herbaceous, a little harsh in an odd chemically way, distinguished in some measure by the unusual character-creating terpene 1,3,8-p-menthatriene, which some are calling cooling by which they mean effusing coolness, and some regard as woody or exuding an effect of oiliness, backed up in turn by the phenolic ether myristicin vibrating at a frequency that registers warm and balsamic (it serves the spicy psychoactive jolt in nutmeg oil), and finally the whole integrated accord transitions toward the departing dry-away that drives the rest away as it dispatches fading shades of soapy silage."

Saffron perceives molecular building blocks within combinative clouds of perfume in the way that musicians hear individual tones within a chord. And she associates those compounds in real time with their appearances in other aromatic vapors, in the way that cinephiles recall other projects by actors of a given film.

"No no, nicotine isn't present in these tobacco extracts, nor is it transmitted by this *concrète*, which makes a show of its balmy hereness by giving vapory voice to its straw-like weediness and an agrestic effluence with a dry yet mellifluent element, and by disseminating its volatiles that establish the presence of a figs-and-honey-filled leather-cigar-case construction, nor is nicotine dispensed along with the fumes of formidable fragrantness emerging from the *absolue* being passed around, which is a choice selection from our collection owing to its projection of metabolites that connote a note of chocolate-covered raisins in distinction but linked to a dirty castoreum-like fruity fecal facet, meanwhile we have another sample circulating that conjures olfactive images of heated henna and sour wheat and apricots and dates piled over urine-soaked acetous grass.

Now, there are an additional three thousand compounds that have been positively identified in tobacco foliage, many derived of carotenoid (pigment) oxidative degradation, and many of these are odorfully elicitative, such as the tones of violet-raspberry ionone and minty apple-tea beta-damascone, both well known."

And some additional phrases not found in your Spanish dictionaries: *ajuste de cuentas* indicates revenge or getting even, *ponerse a beber* means hit the bottle. And one more: a *pozolero* has knowledge of chemistry and so becomes responsible in a gang to dispose of bodies (a cynical appropriation of the term *pozole,* which denotes the dear-to-us delectable hominy soup).

"Have you observed that no one honks their horn when driving around here? People are reticent, so as not to chance angering the wrong person?"

Perfumes of Stipulation
(Juniper)

"I'm nearly but not quite prepared to fetch oils for sampling," Saffron announces, then whispers to me, "occupy our guests for a spell?"

A plant perfume. It has no precise boundary, diffusing along a gradient into its environment. And no precise composition, perpetually changing by means of chemical reactions between constituents and surrounding principles. And no precise duration, changing until appearing gone, though the molecules *per se* are often intact, and may conceivably be bearing related or divergent messages in a different context. So perfume is somehow not really delimited or defined, and we can't know precisely where it is or how it works, not in the sense that we can clearly know, say, where a bucket of paint is and how it works.

"Difficult idea?"

Much as it appears that our fellow large-brained beings are incapable of appreciating the distinguishing manners of activities of this queer phenomenon we call Life, it would be nice if all our analogizing would actually serve to throw some light on the nature of Living Nature.

"There's an idea."

Barry Lopez describes a river by explaining that it expresses biotic Life in dynamic relation to everything around, like salmon within, violet-green swallows swooping its surface, alder twigs floating in its current, mountain lions sipping its bank water, rock configurations that break its flow, and so on.

"An idea that's been verified."

A plant perfume is like a river, a kind of expression of Life, and of the curious affair of living. The emissive infochemicals are even more alive than a river in certain ways. They're imbued with many inimitable properties of biological organisms, yet not in every respect. So, insofar as we might say that a plant perfume lives, our attribution is qualified by what aspect of Creation we choose to bring into focus.

"Life is like a river, it's such a cliché (albeit, many such truisms happen to be true)."

Contrastingly, industrial odorants are more like many human-designed landscapes, of massive multi-lane intersections that dare someone to act the role of pedestrian, of crowded freeways that dare an animal to try to reach from one side to the next, of monoculture lawns permeated with poison that dare a colonizing weed seed to germinate.

"By true, we mean true to Life."

And those very-dead lifeless really-dead non-living solutions of xenobiotic pollution comprising factory odoraments in synthetic solvents for spraying and smearing on people's skin?—they're suitably sold by retail vendors of inanimateness at outlet centers for ersatzness, and called p-e-r-f-u-m-e-s.

"By truth, we mean what happens to an idea that's been verified by Earthly experience."

And just as a river suffers a dam to generate electricity, plant perfumes are likewise subjected to heedless agents of control, the inherent vital currency surrendering to chemical venturers, the metabolic anarcho-vibrancy subjugated by the scheming censurers. Bottled messages of monotony are consigned to replace wild Nature, degradation to replace gentle domestication, rote reduction to replace mindful time-tested technology.

"There's a difference between a neck massage on the one hand and a prefrontal lobotomy using a chisel through the eye socket."

That's another way to put it.

"We're scheduled and ready with juniper oils, to review a few and construe the basis of personal differences, as each panelist is invited to share and compare your private inferences."

"This selection dispenses to our senses an effluvium with the character of a fresh layer of gerbil-cage litter like a persistent presence of pencil shavings like an ambience of woodshop sawdust like a Spanish-cedar cigar box, which then disperses and eventually dissipates into a less brashly diffusive cloud reflecting guaiacwood withering and smoke and tar and cade lingering."

No, not that, not Texas cedarwood, what we anticipate is very different. Rather, ticketed for this panel should be juniper the term regarded colloquially, not just any *Juniper* the Latin identifier.

"This next emanation imparts a sensation recalling reams of dry paper (in relation to the wet-paper vapors expelled by immortelle) stacked upon a clean table of recently milled wood positioned over moist earth, transmitting a resonant smattering of suave sweet-and-sour tonality becoming balsamic on fading?"

No, not Virginia cedarwood either, not that one, what we anticipate is very different. Rather, ticketed for this panel should be juniper the trade and broker's designation, not just any *Juniper* the botanical appellation.

"The next aromatic emission seems to effuse a loose pungent pyrazinic assemblage that's marginally dirty, verdant in the manner of green vegetables, herbaceous in the manner of vegetal galbanum?"

No, not that either, not Spanish savin oil, what we anticipate is very different. Rather, ticketed for this panel should be juniper the common epithet, not just any *Juniper* the taxonomic denomination.

"The bracing body of this next embodiment has a remindful creosote complexion, a wood-fireplace-smoky soapbox for maximal delivery of phenolic declarations, then the dry-away comes on to jar my sensory memory with a property that's chamois-leathery?"

No, definitely not cade oil, which is destructively distilled, not even close, what we anticipate is very different. Rather, ticketed for this panel should be juniper the familiar marketplace entity, not just any *Juniper* the genus name.

"This next elicitative sample gives off piney-turpentiny vapors as if they're lifting from an oak barrel, radiating cineolic traces against a resinous base, with a warm oily footing that dimly references labdanum or something animal like the skin of a mammal?"

Again no, not the Phoenician juniper, which is derived from wood, what we anticipate is very different. Rather, ticketed for this panel should be juniper berry, not just any *Juniper* the scientific label.

No, queued for review, we anticipate, are several oils specified as juniper that are extracted from so-called berries of *J. com-*

munis, not from lumber of heartwood or sapwood or boards or sawdust or twigs or branches or leaves or stumps or logs from any of numerous congeneric *Juniperus*, and not any other kindred or allied oils either, not cedar or cypress or cedarleaf (not *Cedrus, Cupressus, Chamaecyparis,* or *Thuja*).

"Now, this next oil rolls out a terpenic introduction to an olfactive construction that gives regardful props to pine and turpentine and incorporates influences from fresh outdoorsy elements of camphor carrot pepper mint and fir."

Yes, that one.

The berry fruits continue to be harvested and placed into traditional wooden trugs mostly by hand, we understand ... however, in actuality they are neither berries nor even fruits, but rather fruit-scented berrylike seed strobili.

"We call them female cones."

Their turning from green to blue-black indicates a transition within their fleshy tissue, namely the initiation of a noteworthy biosynthetic operation, the creditworthy formation of sugar, which is potential fuel for the fermentation, which is an attention-worthy development often encouraged by praiseworthy producers to precede the distillation in service of the thankworthy production of liquor.

"It's unusual that a raw coniferous fragrant material is put to use as seasoning in northern Europe, to join the ranks of all those spices from warmer climes."

Dominating the composition of most juniper essential oils, as main components, are monoterpenes, especially alpha-pinene, along with myrcene which presents a celery effect, and sabinene which instills a citrus nuance, as well as character-shaping oxygenates such as terpinen-4-ol which contributes a mentholish evocation in its exterior by which we mean anterior though nearer to nutmeg in its interior or you could say posterior.

"Green toppy headnotes of spruce and lemon juice are readily turned loose giving an impression of illumination to the summed bouquet—an effervescent herbal lift, then a heart-note of earth is issued, then a resinous layer, finally a balsamic base-chord is unveiled—the predominant sensory suggestion is of crisp sweetness that flirts with bitterness yet never bittersweetness."

And while copious alpha-pinene is characteristic of juniper, and coniferous plants generally, the volatile compound also acts in diverse minor roles as a trace metabolite in thousands (or more) of diverse plant populations that represent a considerable share of the World's floras, botanical families including those of lovage and lavender, laurel and lemon and a good many others.

"The carbon dioxide extract releases into its enveloping head-space an evergreen aspect that is dry with respect to spiciness (not in terms of wine evaluation in which that attributive con-notes fewer sugars), revealing an organoleptic quality seeming warmer, can I say softer? or richer? maybe smoother and fruitier, yes, with an early-rising sulphury fraction and a pineapple por-tion, a blackcurrant facet and a minor show of vanilla."

Perfumes of Correspondence
(1,8-cineole)

⌘

"In the vital folds of Earthly space and time, 1,8-cineole fulfills its destiny by floating this way and that, transmitting one or another message, materializing here and there, telling some story or the other, all in the service of perfume."

This evening we've prepared a workshop that begins with a *polémica* to inspire some *reflexión* bearing upon the main *instrucción* to be elaborated by *testimonio*.

"Much as 1,8-cineole dances with alpha-pinene which asserts a particularly buoyant cool-tart tone of crushed pine needles, it also mingles with myrtenyl acetate which radiates some furniture-in-the-raw fruitiness, and the components together make up the flowery foliaceousness which is the basis of the myrtaceous odorousness that's hard to nail down yet distinguishes this sample distillate made from glossy leaves of shrubs in Corsica, France," Saffron recites to the group.

Myrtle, yes.

"Then the molecule moves on to reunite with terpene aldehyde safranal with which it tops off a resonant cocktail comprising aroma citations of honey hay tobacco musk leather ozone and almonds which conjointly characterize extracts from hand-harvested crocus style tops and stigmas in La Mancha, Spain."

Saffron, yes, right, as in *azafrán* the high-priced spice.

"Next 1,8-cineole teams up with terpinen-4-ol (of anti-infectious acclaim in the context of tea-tree oil fame) to odorfully augment the lamiaceous leafy exterior afforded by the mass of principles which lastingly exude from populations of Egyptian marjoram."

Now our salon hostess is losing her focus, "They're as porous as coffee filters," referring to the condition and types of sewage pipes around here. Now our salonniere takes up a tangential affair, "The compound indole is floral when weakly concentrated while nauseatingly fecal in high concentration," the topic of the session is transitioning to questions of dilutions of solutions.

Then okay, let that be our segue.

Abridged dictionaries lately include words like *mcdonaldization grobalization coca-colonization* and *walmarting*, terms that bear on the scourge of quantification afflicting modern societies, and the matter of exponential amplification that seems necessary for serious material accomplishment.

"Animals and plants play the same numbers game as we human people the unappeasable?"

Swarms of several hundred thousand army ants readily give up their lives for the benefit of the colony, and weedy dandelions release thousands of winged propagules into the air, and rabbits reproduce ... like rabbits.

"Think of the willy-nilly unpredictability of wind currents evolutionarily trusted to carry microscopic orchid seeds to their perfect new homes for germination."

Yet, the human operation of multiplication turns mere ill will into widespread violation, turns isolated chauvinistic bullying into ethnic cleansing, turns boys with sticks into armed warfare, turns a pogrom into a holocaust, turns some sloppy anthropic solipsism into the wholesale corruption of intricate biological and cultural communities.

"As much as we sapiens are set apart from the rest of Creation, elegant time-honed faculties of organisms in Nature may likewise come under the influence of instrumental mathematics?"

An evident historic break resulted upon the surging ascent of disembedded thought, the propensity among humankind for a kind of distancing deliberation. And so now, here we are, with our bloated brains, foisting on long-established ecologies all sorts of contrived new measures, proposing solutions that are rarely demonstrated to be workable over time, imposing designs with factors and elements in new quantities, adding variables in new-to-Life orders of magnitude, allocating new conditions by means of numerical abstraction.

"To be sure, we hominids are silly in love with disengaged analyses that effect strategies ordained from the top down, by which we mean schemes that are remotely designed."

We extend and multiply and concentrate without any limits whatsoever, to make malignancy from gradual growth, peril from piquance, calamity from high jinks, and obsession from mindful regard, as our accomplishments are context-free, unrestrained and unabated.

"So wave bye-bye to the type of incremental fine-tuning that we're losing, the type aimlessly generated among wild Nature, which we're dooming."

Now guests, we suggest, that you get out your *mouillettes*, inasmuch as, with respect to the nuanced indicators of distress plants express, the next part is the best...

Presently we're queued to experience a blue mallee essential oil (*Eucalyptus polybractea*), of which the oxygenated cyclic monoterpenoid 1,8-cineole is the primary (by its preponderance, constituting up to ninety percent) chemical constituent, thus well suited to help us introduce today's exercise.

"Breezy and drifting and easily lifting, indeed ethereal yet also material, keenly effusive while real and diffusive, but that said, still this selection seems to expand and disband, then clear and disappear."

The characteristic redolence of 1,8-cineole is recognizable in the distillates of many other eucalyptus species. So much so that the molecule is a namesake of the genus ... cineol aka cineole has been denominated *eucalyptol*.

"We mean to say penetrating when we say nare-hair-levitating."

The scent issued by blue gum eucalyptus is ... eucalyptuslike? and that of its volatile oil (the primary industrial source of 1,8-cineole) is ... cineolic?

"Those aren't unreasonable attempts at lyrical depiction of an aromatic emission, using a fragmentary vocabulary that takes us only so far. It is to describe a perfume by making use of a lexical concierge that drops us off at a bus station and says good luck."

This cyclic ether (also considered an oxide) is so ubiquitous in the Natural World that it has engendered the adjective—*cineolic*—to denote the vapory evocation paradoxically both familiar and difficult to pin down. The term *medicinal* provides an idea, however imprecise, which is more than we can say for other attributives that have served efforts at times to relate the odorful impression of eucalyptol: it's not camphorous, not mentholic, not phenolic, not cooling, not thymolic, no not cresylic, and definitely not wintergreen.

"...on the move again, eucalyptol now visits with a family of volatile compounds that collectively constitute a splashing lavandaceous effluvium with coumarinic cut-grass notes radiating from oil extracted by steam stills from spike lavender plants in Spain—"

And neither does our trail of study lead us to the metabolites fenchone or borneol, yet those fragrant agents too have frequently been lumped with and poorly distinguished from eucalyptol. Likewise, sensory associations with candy and toothpaste and chewing gum flavors ... not helpful.

"...now the molecule turns to those eminent thujone isomers, alpha and beta, to assist them in fashioning the bitter-green cutting ketonic quality of mugwort (the moxibustion herb) oil hydrodistilled from whole flowering bushes growing near Katmandu, Nepal—"

As to falsification, the crude eucalyptus oils from which eucalyptol is obtained are commonly adulterated to meet standards, rectification being a routine practice to lift its percentage. However, for a change (though it's hardly consoling), this singular chemical compound, as traded in the marketplace, is not likely to be a product of artificial synthesis but rather an isolate sequestered from plants, mostly eucalypts.

"...eventually the molecule returns to the myrtle family, this time to collaborate with eugenol (which shows up big, to seventy-five percent) on the aroma of pimento berry oil—that's *pimienta dulce*, not *pimiento dulce*, which is sweet paprika, and not *pimienta picante*, which is chili—distilled from unripe fruits of Jamaican trees. This same plant also goes by the designation *allspice*, an appellation that derives from the common observation that its perfume evokes a combination or at least a scentful approximation of nutmeg and clove and cinnamon—"

With a measure of vapor pressure that's through-the-roof, the molecule is, poof, raring to lift off, in no time it's aloft, like a thrusting rocket of volatiles, puff, to meet your inhalation, to waft into your pharynx, then another step to pass through and it's deep inside you, the large surface area of your lungs intimately connected by alveoli to your circulatory system, for travel with blood to close and far bodily destinations.

"Authors of books on *aromathérapie* reference the circulation of cineole with the analogizing notion of wind in motion."

Over three hundred species of eucalyptus indigenous to Australia harbor essential oil within their foliage, and from one to the next, eucalyptol helps shape fragrant character:

"…adds that trademark cineolic theme to the otherwise soapy stream of borealic and metallic effects exhibited by blue mallee oil drawn from coppiced trees down under, and influences in like manner the winey piney and camphory gully gum (blackbutt) oil from trees in South America which dispatch a batch of catty blackcurrant-patch principles as well, and bares additionally a reserved activity in lemon-scented ironbark oil from trees in Brazil (try to taste the lime backnote after inhaling), then combines with piperitone to give a lemony fresh-blowy mint-like flourish to the distillate of narrow-leaved (black) peppermint eucalyptus trees in New South Wales, and delivers also a subtle inkling like a cineolic sprinkling to the aldehydic citronellal-rich Guatemalan lemon eucalyptus oil, and instills a prominent fraction to the olfactive action of Tasmanian blue gum trees in China Ecuador Spain and Portugal and elsewhere from which the compound is extensively sourced for Industry, and moreover makes its presence felt among perfumes sent forth from green mallee, camden woollybut, kangaroo island narrow-leaved mallee, blue peppermint, and many more."

Eucalyptol gets around. Whereas the principle may be associated archetypically with the fragrances of eucalyptus plants, it also combines with innumerable (really, we could never number them) volatile metabolites from an unthinkable number (really, we can't think of the number) of different species.

"…then joins with a herd of herbful alpha-terpinyl acetate in contribution to the glowing gingery scents of Sri Lankan cardamom oil, and subsequently links up with the ketones pino-camphone and isopinocamphone now to be found within a combinative compound scentingly sending out minty esteric (clary-like) elicitations (revealed also among headspace vapors of chartreuse liqueur) which etherealize and then materialize upon the distillation of hyssop perennials cultivated in Hungary."

Impressive, the multitude of settings and circumstances in which eucalyptol turns up.

"We've barely made a dent. Checking our list, the case histories become more interesting—next up for review are perfume orchids that pass eucalyptol along to pollinating euglossine bees who incorporate the molecule in their proprietary reproductive biology."

And there's galangal. And spearmint. And thyme.

"And rosemary black pepper basil and tea tree, oregano star anise ginger and ho leaf, bay laurel peppermint kitchen sage and atlas cedar, Syrian rue southernwood and winter savory … surely there are thousands of unique biotic expressions wherein eucalyptol serves in some role as an element of fragrant messaging."

In large numbers, yet not necessarily playing the numbers as we insatiate sapiens.

Perfumes of Conquest
(Bay Laurel)

Jean-Claude Ellena, the renowned obi-wan kenobi of fragrance, says that his perfumes are like illusions, which are like dreams, which are always more beautiful than reality.

"No latecomers are expected to show, none that I know, I don't think so."

I don't deny it, how very turned off I am to that boastful club of crusaders against Nature, those overachieving line cooks who deracinate perfumed songs of Life in favor of fumes that fan their ego fires.

"Some say *laurier* or Grecian laurel while others say bay, or sweet bay, we are nonetheless confident to say that the extracts being gathered and assembled are all evolutionary expressions of a common design, each a distinct portrayal of the conforming character of bay laurel."

The feathers in their caps are made of synthetic textiles and the notches in their belts are etched by innovative mechanical gizmos.

"It is to *Laurus nobilis* that we are referring, the iconic plant of Greek and Roman lore."

I'm still unnerved to read Stephan Jellinek exuberate about the supposed thirty-two year renaissance for perfumery, the original stretch of big-time lab-made molecule development from 1899 to 1921, that exceeded all aesthetic progress of the preceding four thousand years—why? because finally, sophisticated harmonies of artistic creation began to replace simple harmonies of Nature—he wrote that—what an allegation, my heart sinks to think of it.

"We've all heard about the gods Asclepius and Apollo and the wreaths of honor made from sprigs of laurel branches."

That such and corresponding views have seeped into the common mind is maybe owing to the expansive reach of an empire in which the authentic is trumped by prosthetics and synthetics, and mathematical man proclaims himself God, ordaining reasons for the counterfesance.

"And we've heard about the Delphic priestesses and the derivation of the term *baccalaureate*."

How shall we push back? against those fraternal brothers of the fraudful cult of chemical reduction? those cunning up-and-coming self-loving committed hyper-witted movers and shakers, being haters of plant perfumes and makers of mass perfumes? those remorseless—

"We'll be launching momentarily."

The last hundred and fifty years of depersonalized violence have constituted the bloodiest span of history since the advent of Life on Earth, taking up after the inviolable Enlightenment laws of Kepler and Galileo and Newton, which seeded the dispassionate systems of control now reigning in corporate boardrooms, laboratories and university classrooms, and chemical factories—

"Today's samples are pulled and prepared," this time Saffron flat out triggers me—

Wait, I won't be censored, thank you, when I say what I want, which others won't, or at least don't, which is … that the explosive proliferation of chemical innovation was linked hand-in-hand to the escalation of wars and wholesale degradation of Nature, as over a hundred thousand novel laboratory substances have since been introduced into our environments, to set off endless poorly-understood cascades of effects, the compounds announcing themselves as markers in blood and breast milk of Inuit Eskimos and Japanese cormorants and Mongolian children and Arctic polar bears, as meanwhile America's brightest physicists were promiscuously concocting nuclear communiqués tailored to peel the skin from the faces of millions of unlucky victims of human ingenuity—

"The test strips are imbued and waiting."

…as aroma houses were concurrently gobbled up by chemical concerns, that celebrated with a party of bingeing, of ransacking and pillaging native plant communities, upon which the precocious so-called fathers of modern perfumery wetted their pants over promise of possibilities and riches from cheap synthetic odoraments, and I'll name perpetrators, I don't care, like Jordi-Pey, Laporte, Guerlain, Roudnitska, Carles, Beaux, Coty, Grojsman, Alméras, Robert, and many others likewise neomanic—

"The *mouillettes* are dipped and ready."

…who with crooked smiles and contrived sensibilities have led a relentless series of charged assaults against the wonders of Earthly splendor, against the ecologically embedded and epic-time-tested, the subtly sensible and sensual, the wild and improbable, the vital yet vulnerable, the overrun and under siege, struggling silently to stay free.

"The *touches à sentir* have been spotted with essential oil."

The emperors are wearing no clothes? The self-satisfied perfumers have been satisfying themselves at parties, cocksurely and compulsively laughing and lying at multicultural orgies, hosted early on by the Egyptians and Babylonians, the Chinese and Greeks, Romans and Arabs, eventually by the French and Germans, then Russians and Americans.

"The vapors are already lifting."

The bloodiest conquests were carried out by perfumers, marauding horsemen were perfumers, high-seas pirates were perfumers, natural diverseness was flattened out by perfumers, the planet prospected and ravaged by perfumers, primeval areas desecrated by perfumers and can't be restored, communities robbed by perfumers, slaves taken by perfumers, child soldiers conscripted by perfumers, indigenous cultures blighted by perfumers, rituals myths legends languages and dialects all decimated by perfumers.

"Presently we're pleased to present bay laurel, our volatile yet constant friend and ally. The tree is kin to some other famous faces of the Lauraceae, namely cinnamon and avocado, sassafras and rosewood and may chang too. With its freewheeling cinnamic notes and difficult-to-domesticate eugenol, it does what it can to resist, to buck the trend, to take exception."

So, I'm guilty of some innocent hyperbole? But I take biotic cleansing personally, take the plight of Life earnestly, take to heart the denaturation of Nature, the negation of Creation, take the siege seriously. I know it sounds over-the-top, so I'll now stop, to revisit the violations later, in the matter of the chemical makeover being prosecuted by corporate perfumers.

"The opening evocation registers as vernally fresh and dulcifying in a shallow-lying eucalyptish sort of way, much as a balmy naturalness sits over a soft balsamic undergirding, soon succeeded by a terpenic lauraceous herbaceousness," Saffron has previously distributed the flight of samples, this first being a Corsican distillation.

The bay laurel that grows along Mediterranean coasts is not to be confused with the confamiliar California laurel, an *Umbellularia* dubbed headache tree by those who've suffered the effects of the monoterpene ketone umbellulone that is contained within the clouding emission of the volatile oil. Nor is bay laurel to be mistaken for West Indian bay, a myrtle-family *Pimenta* in service to making bay rum cologne. Nor with cherry laurel, a rose-family *Prunus* harboring a concerning fraction of prussic acid.

"The main component, 1,8-cineole, appears during springtime to spike in concentration, swelling especially among North African populations."

Newly dunked blotter strips are being exchanged, swinging around the table . . . a sample from Turkey, another from Bosnia and Herzegovina. These particular batches of infochemicals are not likely to have been messed with, having bypassed the expectable manipulation of the impostrous Fragrance Industry.

"The assorted variety impart a subtly antiseptic ambience of camphor—the overall influence can be emotionally narcotic—the nicest drydowns are creamy—the Spanish wafts penetratingly cineolic like cajeput—the Cretan connotes a grove of clove trees scattered with anise seeds and tangentially projects a deep-set rosy aspect."

Dry slight fragrant spice, nice, arriving and tailing with tickling spiciness ... attenuated peppery top-notes of spice, nice, reminiscent of the modest manner by which cardamom bestows spiciness ... the middle section liberating a cinnamon-like impression of spice, nice, masculine by its assertive spiciness...

Perfumes of Conveyance

Sadists are subject to cultural preferences just like anyone. In Africa, machetes are used to amputate mostly arms and legs, while Guatemalan commandos are inclined toward castration, but Mexican *sicarios* are partial to decapitation.

"Presently it's the dry season, so *ladrilleros* are working around the clock to manufacture bricks, and collecting different dirts along with organic matter such as sawdust or cow or goat (not horse) manure to reduce the weight and limit cracking of the molded forms, which are baked thousands at a time in large subsurface kilns," Saffron explains.

There's a new mayor in town. The last *jefe* ran into trouble, they say, with some constituents, who crushed his hands and feet with an iron bar, then burned his face with cigarettes, then used the bar a second time to knock out his teeth.

"But there's not much wood around here, so the brickmakers burn what they find: electronic equipment, old computers, dirty motor oil, anything to entertain the *quema* for a while. This includes refuse from garbage trucks bound for the landfill, as the drivers save money when their trip to the dump is diverted. Yet that arrangement isn't ideal, insofar as the *ladrilleros* can't process the entire mess of organic debris."

Each time one of the street kids disappears, the others insist that he went to live with his uncle. It's as if they're all instructed to repeat this line. But there is also whispering in the *barrio* about body-organ contraband abductions, that such heists are lucrative and happening more commonly, they (psst) say.

"The brickmakers pick up tires from local *vulcas*, and the *nylo* (nylon) imparts a desirable reddish hue to the *ladrillos*, they say. Whereas the good color is also obtainable from sawdust, the truckers hauling *alamo* (cottonwood) construction waste from Michoacan sawmills have lately raised their prices, on account of *cobros de piso* (extortion payments), they say."

During rush hour on a main thoroughfare in Boca del Rio, Veracruz, thirty-five corpses were thrown onto the pavement. They were naked, bloody and bound and showed signs of extreme torture, with the words *por-z* scrawled across their bodies. The people murdered were chosen at random by killers in order to send a message. Just a message.

"... whoosh, pass the message—the monoterpene gamma-terpinene plays a role in aromatic dispatches by so many types of plants, the number is surely composed of six figures (oh, animals too, apologies to brown loopers and larch beetles, pine moths and European rabbits), yet its olfactive contribution is possibly minuscule or minor or occasionally influential, sometimes artifactual upon hydrodistillation, in any case the compound expresses an herby terpenaceous tone that's not much but at least a touch less rutaceous (lemony) than its sister-isomer the alpha version and as such is well represented in glandular leaf trichomes of savory lantana oregano tarragon rosemary marjoram thyme and tea tree, and makes a hesperidic statement albeit short-lived (bearing little tenacity) and less prominent (in smaller concentration) when taking part as a component of ajowan cumin angelica juniper nutmeg and coriander essential oils, its presence so slight in a population of clary sage in Turkey as to be undetected, these same plants emitting an abundance of—psst, pass the message—"

The fires go for fifteen hours or more, but the toxic vapors early on are most violently combusting and visibly flaring up, thus the burn is ignited soon after sunset. At the outset, packaging for kindling and other various *combustibles* are piled up beside the *horno*. The *rojo vivo* (denotes the degree of redness indicating optimal heat) marks the initiation upon which plumes of black smoke are generated under cover of darkness.

"Nighttime burning is the worst, as the discharging fumes leave their point of origination and flow like a river, near the ground because of nocturnal temperature inversions, meandering about the very places that animals and people dwell, which is unfortunate since the streaming gases are often poisonous combustion products of perfume incineration."

Noxious vapors aside, these boxed flacons of mephitic fragrances in alcohol are hardly well-suited as fuel for brickmaking ovens since they become pressurized because of the tightly fitting caps, which eventually propel off with explosive force. But the options of *ladrilleros* are limited, we suppose.

"...whoosh, pass the message—the verdant blossomy terpenoid ester linalyl acetate, which proportionally dominates the oils of those Anatolian salvias while being most renowned for shaping, along with the corresponding monoterpenol linalol, the esteemed extractive perfumes from lavender plants, so much so (insert sad-faced emoticon here) that numerical percentages of these two components among other volatile metabolites are criteria measured by chemical brokers and compared (the higher the ester the better) against standard values, but be that as it may, when considered on its own, it is the most elicitative a-la-cart part of the terpy-tart seemingly fruit-infused citrus-imbued molecular signal notably broadcast by horsemint and orange (especially bergamot orange) peels and twigs and leaves (namely petitgrain) and flowers (principally neroli), even showing up in some labdanum distillates, a modicum also contained within scented transmissions lifting from botanical communities dominated by sweet marjoram, along with—muah, pass the message—"

"Your face is full of life—that's what a hitman who works around here is known to say, before he mutilates the faces of his victims with muriatic acid.

Perfumes of Conjugation

"This is a prelude to an *étude*," Saffron initiates the session.

The following class concerns behaviors of aromatic substances *integral* and fractured. In particular, we'll carry over from a recent salon, the surmise of an ether alliance involving basil.

"...like an orientation in formulation."

To begin, we backtrack, to recall the amicable, even harmonious basil-tarragon rapport as resulting from a couple of volatile phenylpropanoid molecules that characterize the elicitative perfumes broadcast by both of these herbs—the subtly so-so spiced-tea warmed-earth character of methyl eugenol tags along the welcoming anise-fennel persona of methyl chavicol to create an emergent phenyl methyl ether spice-box effect.

"...or a special lesson calling into question certain suggestions as to blending essential oil expressions."

Yet, while the scentful secretions of sweet basil and tarragon snuggle up together in Nature, they are prone to kick the evocative tone of wormwood out of their accordant communal bed. So then, who do you suppose might facilitate an alliance between these conflicting emissive camps?

"...really, it's more testimony in the manner of a ceremony."

The nature of spike lavender is to act as an olfactively amiable *interlocuteur*, a congenial middleman, for it shares with sweet basil and tarragon the phenylpropene methyl chavicol (also the oxide 1,8-cineole and the monoterpenol linalol) and shares with wormwood the ketone camphor. So it serves to bridge a gap, like Janus the Roman god of doorways and passages and molecular linkages, to mediate an aesthetic transaction among odor principles.

"Like an arbiter of situational differences."

In this way, expressions comprising basil and tarragon with wormwood and spike lavender may roll around together, without adversarial behavior—no more exclusive chemical cliques.

"Like a go-between across conditional interfaces."

In any case, I wonder about the fractional composition of these metabolic medleys, namely those incorporating linalol, which is so neighborly that it good-naturedly plays the part of peacemaker more often than not. Perhaps it's for this reason that linalol is more generously represented among botanical perfumes as compared to its prickly pungent partners?

"Shall we put the thesis to a test?" Saffron whispers loudly.

And whereas methyl eugenol might make up to fifty percent of the vapors emanating from populations of certain basil cultivars, it contrastingly assumes the role of minority constituent in most messaging transmissions of plants, such as those from pimento clove laurel allspice and bay, and additionally in emissions of rosemary ylang verbena rose and even certain citrus. And while minor eugenolic influences may be sensorially pleasing (so we're perceiving), the essence of such a lesser presence is that it's not seeming to be distinguishably spicy or spice-breathing.

"On display is the interplay of divergence and likeness."

And much as we find many of the same chemical components at front edges of distinct courses of genealogical descent, these identical compounds originate independently.

"Linalol, for example, is all over the map (of phylogeny)."

And bear in mind, linalol doesn't navigate about environments on its own, rather it counts only as one component, in active and interactive relation with others, moving through worlds as part of an agglomerated whole, an individual among many in a series of chemical suites intact, among animated collective units of metabolites, each communicating with a melded voice.

"No one debates over the open-and-shut case of whether biosynthetic pathways have stable states."

Just as the beak of a cormorant, stamen of a salvia, insectivorous mechanism of a bog plant, pouch of a wallaby, and jaw of an alligator are each one morphological feature of a congruent complex, so too are distinct volatiles part of an aromatic ensemble, a composite perfume, reflecting a long elaborate evolutionary history, a course associated with discarded patterns and forms, countless scrapped solutions and rejected compromises and failed settlements.

"Notwithstanding three billion years of Life's intricate lessons, the rich tapestry of Creation reflects an incomprehensible integrity."

The fluxing nature of such molecular assemblages doesn't lend itself to comprehension by means of analytical tools, such as mass spectrometry. And for all the separating and consolidating, the contextual shapeshifting, nonetheless our attention is fixed on just an instantiating slice, like a snapshot, only a brief stretch during the fluid transitioning, or eventual departure, of the infochemical agents of things (like plants) that are living.

"So, put away those white lab coats, rid yourself of the reductive baggage, and make peace with the vital carriage of compressed information traded among biotic beings on Earth."

The bundled formations of coordinated metabolic improvisation that exist in the world of our experience have emerged upon eons and eons (and counting) of never-ending trials, of sifting and culling, auditioning and selecting, scrambling and fixing. Our aromatic contemporaries are derived from such processes, as are the negotiated relationships between them. The perfumed landscapes of Living Nature are nothing if not the result of myriad compacts spanning the history of Life.

"But there are loose threads that hang from the frayed fragrant fabric of Life, and never a lack of luminaries ever eager to give a tug."

Perfumes of Exploit

Saffron, why not start a cult? with you as the guru? who will get your vital message across by eliminating, one after another, the various media of communication? with you as the leader of a new hermetic sect that will practice the abstemious self-discipline of shutting down exposure to external information? aimed at purifying the means by which the World is perceived? so therefore, there will be no writing, no music, no speaking, no facial expressions (you'll wear a burqa), leaving in the end, only that currency of information that no one can deny, not while they still live ... perfume.

"At issue are chemical tricksters egged on by their *perfumista* sisters with the encouragement of art-school hipsters."

In the matter of standardized commercial fragrances, let's take a moment, before we proceed, to warn against, or should we just mourn, their preponderance?

"It is so enacted by the fraternity of biophobic perfumers whose naked mission is to abolish whatever is indigenous and undomesticated within their reach, anything truly alive."

They conceive of a world with no idiosyncratic contexts and no incomparable idiosyncrasies, no irrepressible particularities no irreplaceable ecologies and no one-and-only realities, no improbable impracticalities or impractical improbabilities, no unique communities no unpredictable situations no situational sensibilities no vital versions of inimitability and no extraordinary expressions of vitality.

"They are headquartered in abstraction town just next to virtual-ville which is located within counterfeit county in the state of reduction set inside their anything-goes-if-you-can-get-away-with-it world which exists as a mere speck in the nothing-matters-anyway universe."

Apparently, there was another massacre in Mexico of vulnerable migrants? Several managed to survive by feigning death and provided a detailed account of the killing: how they were tied up and told to keep their heads down, heads always down, no eye contact, never any eye contact.

"No personal accounts, no special histories, no singular stories, no differentiating personalities, no recognition of their individuality. No brothers no sisters no mothers no fathers. Only numbers, categories and stripes, as in kinds or types, as in groups and nationalities."

One of the killers ran out of bullets so he finished the job by breaking open some heads with construction debris.

"What? another waxy mass? like the last? (which was guaiac-wood)—no, these are Bulgarian distillates or extracts of zdravetz (zadravets, from an actual *Geranium*, as distinguished from geranium, derived from *Pelargonium*)—we have several samples to serve as examples of the sesquiterpene ketone germacrone, of which the scentless crystalline phase issues with a greeting as it melts upon gentle heating, to reveal a lasting dimensionality with a minty tonality and an herbal florality, though this quality is tricky to single out in reality—a hint of tobacco plus an estery tinge of clary are let off ahead, before settling on a bed of Kazanlik roses—showing with a pinch of broom? detect the oozing influence of orris? exhibiting a warmly woody under-structure?—this displays a slight fleck of pepper and a light spray of hay (all elegantly melding) with a summating dry-away resembling Chinese geranium."

Good for you, industrial enterprisers, that it's too late now for farmhands to go back to farming, that peasants can't regain possession of their knowledge and lands and livelihoods, that many populations have been displaced, such as those of north-ern Mexico. And good for you, top corporate executives, that they make a giant pool of unemployed potential recruits for you to prey upon, and good for you, chief officers and directors seated in boardrooms, that the young among them are demoral-ized about their prospects, susceptible to your pitches. However, they're also open to other offers, including those of organized crime, whose pay and benefits are competitive, and so criminals unsurprisingly make up the new social class around here. So, good for you, big businessmen, that you know what you're doing.

"Phew, fumes of dirty caramelic coffee—it's a grassy spicy brew—throwing out celery-like volatile compounds—it's a meat-and-milky stew—enveloped by a cloud of burnt sugar—so, as it turns out, those odorfully mysterious maple-syrupy vapors that occasionally drift over New York City? come from a nearby factory that processes fenugreek, the Old World legume whose seeds release when crushed a soupy proteinaceous sweet couma-rinic perfume—extraction is usually by alcohol or supercritical carbon dioxide to sequester the starring molecule, the potent lactone sotolone, responsible for the emanation (bizarre) that lingers like creamy curry forever on the *mouillette*."

There is much more to go (much as I bear this touch of vertigo), there is a lot more for us to show.

"It's getting late."

This is just to say that Life is under siege, and sorry if the repeating seems heavy-handed ... well, no, I'm not sorry, as it requires reminding, over and over, the awareness we draw from these vaporous expressions of Creation, that everything organic and wild and vulnerable is being designedly smothered by humanity, but we're not going along, we're not following.

Perfumes of Violation
(Rose)

(Saffron, to initiate the salon, taps a spoon *clink-clink* to the side of a Bordeaux glass.)

Plants cultivated in the Struma Valley, at the foot of the Balkan Mountains, yield the inimitably treasured Bulgarian damask rose otto, notable for its scented symphony of finely cleaved nuances, many fleeting, and the exalting bouquet with its persistent sensuous sublayer summoning a sense of civet or some such suggestion, buoying an expansive and deep-honeyed heart, girded somehow harmoniously by a delicate effervescence, an exterior of pineapple and pepper notes, an enhancement of wet straw and wine tones, the whole perfume attributable to over two thousand (arguably) distinct molecular components (many unidentified), which often combine with ensembles of other fragrant compounds to become agents in unique contexts elsewhere in Nature.

"Such a rich vital pageant, how did it happen? and who could have imagined? the door to deep mystery as so wide open?"

But the cagey counterfeiters of modern perfumery consistently ignore the scope and nature of this involvement of metabolic messaging, willfully miss the point of the real-Life intricacy, pay little attention to why such chemical communiqués and elicitative bulletins are patched together as they are, and discount the situational manner by which this manifold currency is traded and distributed throughout the Natural World.

"They who are sensually stoic, who tune out the way that aroma principles are transmitted in concert, they who are phytophobic, are deaf to the aspect in which plant perfumes are symphonic, in a way that's different from chords of music."

Chemical communication lends itself to composite dispatches. And complicated combinatorial messages are complicated further by complex synergistic effects involving beholders. So we've not a chance to conceive of all the combinations of indications including our reactions to the cues and signs in Nature. An audit would be unmanageable, even unimaginable.

"A zebra combines gestures to express emotion: hostility by flattening back ears, friendliness by pointing them upward, the intensity of either posture measured by ... the degree to which the mouth is open? So when these striped horses feel frisky, their mouths spring gaping wide, a straightforward if not obvious behavioral deployment?"

We gather (from biology literature) that the total chorus of signals that may potentially be conveyed by a composite message is the power set of components, which equals the sum of all possible combinations of subsets.

"Much as that mathematical equation is merely theoretical, it still calls for us to bear in mind, as a frame of reference."

I find the calculation to be adequately intimidating given that most vapors emitted from plants are composed of dozens, often hundreds of discrete chemical petitions, each elaborate transmission comprising numerous metabolic factors to advance whichever mission.

"Rev up your odor decoders, as now we arrive at the moment of Earthly truth."

Samples are presently circulating of rose extracts, for us to register likenesses and contrasts, differentiate between fragrant agents, spot scentful spotlights, and make out the evaporative evolution of traces as revealed from the launching pads of designated cardboard strips:

"You'll notice, upon initial imbuing, early flourishes may appear fresh (limonene?) and fatty (nononal?) with a seeming bolus of *bois de rose* (linalol?), then a tide of dried rose petals (phenyl ethyl alcohol?) that also brings waves of geranium (cis rose oxide?) grass (nerol oxide?) and bitter orange peel (trans rose oxide?), later a development of woodiness (terpinene-4-ol?) waxiness (decanal?) and a splashing arrival of florality (citronellol? strong), then shades of sour lemons (geranial?) neroli (nerol?) and cloves (eugenol?) succeeded by references to plums (trans damascenone?) tea (methyl eugenol?) and redolent roses (geraniol?), next may be accents of apple pie (beta-damascenone?) and blackcurrant (beta-damascone?), a sprinkling of spices (beta-caryophyllene?) a spray of muguet (farnesol?) and a subliminal yet decided presence of pineapple (ethyl hexonate?)—everyone following along? hang on, we've several hundred more principles to identify."

Among aromatic plants, hundreds of familiar molecules are regularly shuffled about here and there, in endless series of metabolic lineups. With each integrated volatile expression, each novel configuration, each one-of-a-kind jumble of juxtapositions, individual constituents renounce their independent identities in favor of a new collective, voices of singular atomic bonds sing in polyphonous unison to create new matchless messages of Creation.

"The proliferation of composite communications of multifold meaning."

And rose perfumes of commerce (where to begin)?—the fetishistic affair of Sophia Grojsman with suffocating synthetic ionones is exhibited vividly by her archetypal rose violation *Paris* by Yves Saint Laurent, the woody rose violation *Une Rose* by Frédéric Malle is a cynical rendition connoting cat pee formulated in the lab, the suitcase-heavy rose violation *Joy* by Jean Patou debases the idea of organic luxury, the choking powdery rose violation *Lipstick Rose* by Frédéric Malle aspiringly mimics fumes of cheap toiletries, the insecticidal rose violation *Nahéma* by Guerlain is claimed (boastfully) to be devoid of any trace of a substance harvested from genuine rose blossoms, the caustic fizzy rose violation *Quel Amour!* by Annick Goutal poses as a gas-station air freshener, the artificial peppery rose violation *Parfum Sacré* and the toothache-sweet rose violation *French Cancan* both by Caron ... well, we can continue on, all day.

"The noxious aldehydic rose violation *Chanel No. 5* was fabricated by Ernest Beaux, who has never been challenged to face his victims."

The idea of femininity expressed by the terpenic rose violation *Rosa Flamenca* by Les Parfums de Rosine, it's the type that might likewise be related by a sex doll. And that of the gourmand rose violation *Ombre Rose* by Charles Brosseau, related by a date rape drug.

"Lastly, as our endeavor to provide a measure of pleasure, we're serving a blended libation crafted of *Elisir di Rose*, an uncommon cordial made from Italian gallic roses, with a chilled *Moscato d'Asti* from northwest Italy. You'll observe how fine bubbles escaping from the effervescing white wine provide lift to the rosaceous elements, propagating a balanced airborne headspace bouquet that evokes the sensation of an ambient perfume beheld by standing midway between a rose garden and a fruit orchard."

Insofar as these herbal cocktails tend to relax the tongue, please remember that this isn't a social event.

Perfumes of Service

"Art is long and life is short."

Human perspiration affiliates with seaweed and sandalwood, some girls expire honey and clary and clover, in adolescence begins the phase of galbanum and opopanax, doors of ambrette and vetiver will open, eventually self-assurance leads the way to cumin and orris and valerian, to the reminiscing of vanilla and almond meal.

"But art that endures is inert."

We have planned for this evening testimony concerning the integration of art and life, art and work, the imaginary and real, fantasy and fact, intellect and instinct.

"We will call to your attention, or at least mention, the malicious convention of relegating art to certain forms made with certain media in certain places to be carried out by certain chosen people," Saffron welcomes everyone.

Pardon me this preamble to point out that a straight line runs through...

...through wanna-be lords of Nature including Francis Bacon (Nature must be bound into service and made a slave) through René Descartes (we render ourselves masters and possessors of Nature) through Edward Teller (we'd be unfaithful to the tradition of Western civilization if we fail to increase man's control over Nature) through—

…through ruthless conquistadors of medieval crusades through massacres of Armenians through slaughtering Native Americans through berserk yet rational Nazi operations through taking of African slaves through all the blood-drenched imperial bloodlust and blood-soaked colonization and bloodthirsty administration of bloody empire through—

"It should be plain to recognize, when we meet with it in whichever guise, whether material or ethereal, rooted or lifting, fluid, drifting, fixed, flowing, mixed, going, coming or running … whichever."

…through Arthur Clark (the dullards may remain on placid Earth and real genius will flourish only in space) through—

…through corporate media moguls through environment pillagers through messianic ministers through neomanic inventors through amoral investors through merciless traders through indifferent innovators through natural resource raiders and their lobbying collaborators and all the Nature negators and depreciators through—

"It's not a connecting line that's unbending, but rather a sinuous track that's unending."

…through Exxon's desecration Monsanto's contamination Amazon's domination Koch Industries' predation Citigroup's accumulation through deep-space exploration through virtual reality through the immorality of industrial farms through Madison Avenue advertising agencies (Daddy, what's the moon supposed to advertise?) through—

…through Perfume Industry icon Paul Jellinek (the sophisticated harmony of artistic creation has replaced the simple harmony of Nature) through—

"…through neo-isms and post-isms and poly-isms and pseudo-isms and the incident schisms in art—"

Forgive me this excursus, but works of art are prone to be separated, sorted, and catalogued by genre into a seeming limitless register of forms. And much as the public is massaged and assuaged, once in a while (all right, true, it's uncommon, yet still) a characteristic style develops with no commercial angle whatsoever, as a school for inquiry into the nature of things, a means to pierce the veil of consensus reality.

"The great bloody and bruised veil of the World."

But a corresponding lineage among perfumers? a comparable earnestness among specialists in modern perfumery? who guilefully falsify natural expressions? who will hide the vintage Bordeaux, hand you a glass of grape Kool-Aid and prod bottoms-up? who will sell you anything, even the rain and claim authorship? who will sell you rain contaminated and claim advancement?

All right, bravo, now this lexical word game: identify the unknown olfactive attribute—I'll provide names of exemplifying botanical materials as hints—ready?—starting with … a cut cucumber—"juicy? dewy? sappy? verdant? vernant? vernal? leaflike? leafy? leavy? airlike? airy? airish? vapory? ozonic? umm, honeydewy? watermelony?" no, how about … violet—"powdery … no? muted? dainty? dusty? chalky? iridaceous …" what?—"irislike?" no-no, I'm referring to the leaf—"herblike? herby? herbous? herbal? herbose? herbaceous? vegetal? vegetative? vegetational? veggieish? green … yes, definitely green," no, let's try—

Perfumery too is subject to sorting, the divisions more akin to genres than styles of pictorial art. Fragrance families may be designated leather or oriental, marine or floral, citrus or chypre or *fougère*. As with other kinds of art, popular fragrances reflect that popular preferences are commonly canvassed and appeased, but moreover, perfumery serves exclusively as a vehicle to please, of commerce or control (both) by degrees—who disagrees?

"Sr. Jellinek, thank you for (freeing us by) severing our ties, to those waters and lands and unprogrammed skies, which have since antiquity been characterized, by intricate volatile fragrant surprises (elaborate scented unexpected prizes)."

They say that we should submit to their technological dream, surrender to their contrived synthetic delusion.

"They say that we should hold still as they shove breathing tubes down our throats, and when it feels as if our tracheae are constricting, we shouldn't worry, that the feeling will pass. They say that the pharyngeal gag reflex can be overcome."

That line … that runs through one factor or another, surely doesn't bypass the world of art, which as an institution shares unity of purpose and endorses the long preoccupation of humanity with mastery over Nature. The art establishment throws in with everyone else in advancing the denial of organic complexity, the subjugation of wild things, and the appointment of artificial surrogates and substitutes for natural substances and processes.

…elemi—"resinous? resiny? no, piney? pitchy? pinesappy? pineneedly? oh, peppery … no? balsamic? balsamous? tart? tangy? terpenic? terpeney? terpenaceous? thuriferous? lemony? lemonzesty?" no, try … cabreuva—"a wood, right? it's woody …" nope—"cool? coolish? suave? suavy? anisic? aniseedy? oh, smoky…" no, let's say … mimosa—"ahh, the sweetest of acacia tree blossoms, honeyed…" no—"what? flowery? floral? labile? wafty? creamy? silky? mellifluous? mellifluent? what, no? mimosoid…" uh-uh, say—

"The most celebrated art tends to be both numbing and up and coming."

But the role for artists has not been as marauding horsemen, rather it has been to fulfill a substitutive mission, a sort of supportive function, to fashion a distraction, that is, to retain creative consignments to serve the powerful, like jesters of medieval royal courts.

"The point of art is palliation to head off our alienation."

Art doesn't disappoint, even though attitudes and conventions may change. Art persists to spare our hearts from breaking, to keep our minds off the existential aching.

"Art always comes through to cover, for those working to subdue or smother, the variousness of Creation."

... laminaria—"huh?" seaweed—"oh, the beach ... no, benthic? benthonic? planktonic? pelagic? thalassic? aquatic?" getting closer, but—"iodinous? rancid? brackish? briny? maritimey? saline? piscine?" no no, let's try ... lavender—"lavandaceous..." uh-uh—"what? cineolic? linalolic? mentholic? menthaceous? camphoraceous? camphorous? camphory? estery? esteric?" nope, imaginative effort though, consider—

Art has never had teeth to sway the disruption of the global climate or the clear-cutting of old-growth forests or the depletion and poisoning of aquifers or the dumping of biomedical toxic trash or the spiking extinction of species or the systematic erosion of topsoils or the production of radioactive waste or the discarding of agricultural heritage or the melting of ancient Siberian peat bogs or the decimation of amphibian populations or the destruction of unique animal and plant communities and ecologies of Life. Or anything.

"When indigenous cultures are ravaged, art thrives."

...clary—"nutty? nutsy? musty? baccy? leathery? tea..." no—
"then, soapy? ambery? earthy? mossy? lichenic?" no, think of
orris—"violaceous? iononic? agrestic? rooty? buttery?" still no,
how about pink grapefruit—"it's crisp and breezy brisk and
sprightly? fizzy pithy sparkling brightly? fleeting blasty fruit
that's fresh? clean crude hesperidic zest ... what no? this play-
ful exercise is impossible, I give up..."

"When uncontrollable Nature is plundered, art thrives."

...wait, just close your eyes, now listen ... think of hydra-
tion or dilution and perspiration and precipitation or baptism
and metabolism or deep-sea divers and steam geysers, think of
a drink and a wash or a swim and a tear, a river clear an oasis
near an ocean blue, think of the morning dew—

"When prairies, rainforests, deserts, woodlands, rivers, and
coastal waters are aggressively prospected, art thrives."

People throughout history and still today are rounded up, bru-
talized and blackmailed and pressured, murdered and tortured
and lynched, but the solitary artist is infrequently herded off,
the outsider artist rarely sent to a gulag or internment camp, the
so-called starving artist seldom in actual fact deprived of food.

"When undomesticable Life is made deficient, art thrives."

After centuries of aspirational art that never much prevailed
upon states of affairs, artworks some generations ago began to be
increasingly severed from the ecologies of Life, less tethered to
our sensual engagement among living Creation, less referential
of our experience as biological beings in the World. Art, for the
most part, has been inert, disassociated from Nature.

"Nice try, Amanda Feilding, with your self-trepanation,
and Zhu Yu, by eating human fetuses, to break from Earthly
insignificance."

Reigning holders of power are primary patrons of the art-makes-a-difference charade. They have little to fear, are rarely fazed, sometimes entertained, and ultimately served by art.

"That line ... runs through ... guess what—I'm steering us back on topic—artful claimants who establish squatters rights on what has become a chemical no-man's land of molecular meaning—of course, perfumers."

Perfumes of Fidelity
(Osmanthus)

⁓⁓⁓

World luminaries have a knack of teasing elemental units into pieces without an idea of putting parts back together.

"Bush, the shock-and-awe braggart?"

I'm thinking of brilliant past-winning humpty-dumpty Nobel laureates such as Philipp Lenard the Nazi physics advisor and Egas Moniz the icepick lobotomist and William Shockley the eugenicist and Henry Kissinger the Cambodia carpet bomber.

"Sorry we're running late, but during the power outage earlier we hesitated to open the fridges stocked with our samples of osmanthus," Saffron says.

I'll take that as my introduction and prompt:

So this salon, this meeting, this evening, its meaning? our intentions? are what? to celebrate fragrance?—actually, no. The aromatic extracts in our queue tell a harrowing story of ravage and desecration—what's to rejoice over? Scent for scent's sake we do not behold. Rather, volatile storytelling metabolites are biologically chosen, organic molecules tailored to chronicle the epic pageant of Creation, to recount the evolutionary drama, to comprise the major messaging medium that so demands to be recognized. These are impactful compounds that take a stand, implore an audience, elicit a response (insistently so), petition living tissue everywhere packed with receptors in waiting. We read the book of Life in its original language, the first edition of the narrative, both visceral and poetic, in which the tragic aspects are most discernible, the central conflict unmistakable. In leading roles are knockoff artists, venturesome counterfeiters of Nature who are sold on the idea of chemical innovation by subverting vital elements of our environments and across the biosphere. Whereas these machinating engineers are unabashed technophiles, they are cagey in how they act upon their biophobic resolve, carrying on like modern-day confidence men, their business omnipresent yet shrouded and ulterior, infiltrating cultures in the grand interest of redesigning Life on Earth. So we consider the fluid portfolios of bundled perfume principles from Nature as emissary teaching tools, testimony of the Natural World, sacraments maybe, rallying cries surely. There'll be no going back for us partisans, awestruck and engaged in this cardinal struggle, enthralled and enlisted in the service of the wild free and vulnerable, authentic expressions of Life in trouble.

"Ready, good ... first helping is an ethanolic wash of osmanthus *concrète*—impressions?—I can make out a subdued emanation of sun-dried apricots—the final-stage exhalation of stewed apricots—the dwindling metabolism of mellow-ripe apricots—a reserved interpretation of apricot jelly? of apricot brandy? a muted representation of an etherealization, which is to say a dematerialization, of apricot nectar?—(we detect a theme here)."

The essential oil of osmanthus features an interesting chemical composition owing to the concentrated dispensation of carotenoid metabolites and the bounty of structurally varied ionone derivatives.

"Add to the apricot compote some plums and figs—and step it up with robust raisins (not prunes)—it asserts an odd accent, something leathery, peculiar, like olives or Roquefort cheese?— also waftingly issues a chord of apian and herbal notes, reflecting wildflower honey—the stone-fruitish radiance is at variance with a minor fragrance of raspberries but nonetheless enables a diffuse dryout that's delicately lactonic, makes sense?"

The extract comes from China, where dried blossoms are famously appropriated to flavor semi-fermented green teas, imparting select perfume principles, like jasmine but fruitier.

"The absolute gives a rosaceous maybe milky maybe ambery ambience—individual principles associated with tobacco and tomato flowers make their distinguishing voices known here—an intense floral flourish comes on recalling the candied come-on of ylang-ylang compounds—all taking place against the effusing backdrop of soothing volatiles alluding to our sense of boronia."

The perfume emitted from actual flowers is difficultly described, elusive in the way that it appears and disappears, ventriloquistic in the manner that it's distinctly perceived some distance away from the plant, radiating with the sun to release lush-and-juicy mature vapors substantially jammy and slightly powdery, strangely ethereal yet penetrating, if that's possible? on account that molecules continue for a time disseminating, we're speculating.

"By the demeanor of the heady transmission, populations of osmanthus bear a sensory resemblance to those of the kindred oleaceous taxa, lilac and jasmine, which is altogether aside from the odorful evocating, errr, evoking of the associated smattering of scentfully diverse shades such as from coconut cassia and citrus, patchouli cedarwood and spiced tea."

Sorry to confirm what you already suspect: that, as is common in modern mass perfumery, the natural material has been rendered an olfactive concept, a Platonic ideal, a category of headspace reconstitutions concocted with lab-made beta-damascenone (roses and plums), beta-ionone (berries and beeswax), gamma-decalactone (peaches and cream), and hedione (jasmine and grapefruits). Sorry to report what you surely expect: that most marketplace materials no longer consist of any substance intercepted from the infochemical communications of genuine living osmanthus plants.

"I believe Calvin Klein *one summer* includes a trace of the natural, something like a homeopathic level."

Not uncommon are such futile attempts to smoothen, so to speak, with irreducible expressions of Nature, the reduced compositions of fragrance formulators, the indelicate migraine-inviting odorous avatars of corporate perfumers.

Perfumes of Possibility

"There is a single chemical compound that exudes from a baby's skull and facilitates bonding with the mother, and a molecule in pumpkin pie that makes men horny," an early-arriving salonist declares matter-of-factly.

Not sometimes not maybe so simple and easy that's that?

As Saffron and I anticipate the arrival of other panel members, she hands me a scintillation vial containing a gourmand blend of cocoa and tea absolutes, carob and coffee tinctures, vanilla oleoresin, a wee trace of bitter almond oil, "We should figure that there is a presence in each of benzaldehyde to bridge disparate elements."

The trail of increasingly complex manifestations of Life, like a silhouette of a migrating heron that slowly disappears into the horizon, at some juncture becomes impossible to follow, our cephalic tissues ineffectual, our best analytical instruments rendered impotent.

"Bye-bye natural laws (good riddance, Nature-dismissive causes)."

Most believe that it's a matter of time before the realm of olfaction, once presumed to be inscrutable, will be mapped out in its entirety. But Living Nature isn't a thing like a dishwasher or smartphone, its operations and patterns never wholly accessible to us. And the insights that are within our reach are to be found in the rearview mirror of Life's procession.

"Hello natural history (welcome, Nature-affirming inquiry)."

All the same, wintergreen emissions consist almost entirely of methyl salicylate, and bitter almond of benzaldehyde, the volatile oils comprising no unnecessary components, bearing no extravagance. There is no beating around the bush, no roundabout aesthetic formulations or convoluted fragrant juxtapositions, only direct unornamented missives that readily waft upon slight heating. Our senses are immediately greeted with the crux of the content, the metabolic message to the point with a sovereign principle, and the dispatch fades as is, without shifting in substance, without transposing to another key, as might be, or segueing to a different motif.

"Some communications are just uncomplicated. The percussive warning of a rattlesnake is concise, economical, and efficient, a straightforward sound to deliver an unequivocal notice."

For animals to enhance or embellish such auditory signals, evolutionary opportunities come and go. In the case of songbird heritage, there are phylogenetic indications of possibilities for singing since way back, when the large low limb of theropods (dinosaurs) on the tree of Life diverged to bear a branch leading to birds which bore a branch leading to passerines which bore a branch leading to various feathered songsters with throat muscles developed to control vocal organs.

"Melodious messages are sent off from denizens of tree branches to others on electric wires and rooftops. Birds sing because they can."

Still, the rattler's rattle is a jury-rigged make-do musical instrument, just as wintergreen and bitter almond are makeshift essential oils. These are stripped-down opportunistic versions of music and perfume.

"Biosynthetic machineries for fragrance-making were in place billions of years ago, then became dormant, then again in the business of adornment, then neglected, then again resurrected?"

Mevalonic and shikimic acid production pathways have been in place for ages to churn out lipophilic bioactive perfumes, but owing to an uneven diversification, we find clusters of chemical complexity within disparate phyletic formations.

"Pockets of elaboration are to be found among conifers and so many angiosperms, namely laurels and labiates, myrtles and roses, gingers and citruses and orchids umbellifers wormwoods and legumes and dogbanes."

Which is to say that real-World evolutionary processes of winnowing and sifting and testing and trying and adapting and filtering and fine-tuning have been erratic.

"Erraticism is a marker of organic evolution."

Perfumes of Advocacy

"When angels ascend to heaven, their beads of sweat drop and germinate as grape vines, after which the perfume of wine has become symbolic," Saffron reads from her journal.

I'm not so sure about the fanciful allegory, yet it has a pleasing ring, oh well.

Saffron introduces tonight's theme, "Like the frenetic whirling of electrons around the cores of two different atoms, concurrently satisfying electromagnetic needs of both, attending to one proton while moonlighting as outer electron shells of others, fragrance assumes a double life as well, enigmatically serving in the separate spheres of substance and idea."

I'm not so sure about the covalent chemical bond metaphor, yet it has a pleasing ring, oh well.

"Perfume fulfills orders in both existential domains, of materiality and poetry, both at once, all the time, all around, all through time."

(Now she summons guests to be seated by tap-tapping her spoon against a brandy glass.)

"Granting that they are memorable, even unforgettable, still I've never in forever been able to remember the Remembrances of Buddha."

The fifth remembrance is pithy and profound: my actions are the ground upon which I stand. Is there any more spot-on line of instruction for living?

I've taken the liberty of adding a sixth: my life is a canvas and my actions are pigmented oils laid down in layers and patterns as my heart dictates. Which is, I suppose, to suggest that one's life is a work of art, each deed a creative improvisation that expresses and reveals.

"In that case, we hope your basis for measuring greatness won't model after the world of art, which is morally weightless."

And a seventh remembrance: my life is a musical composition and my actions are notes and meters that come to me from a mysterious place. Which is, I suppose, to make a point about the ultimately unaccountable nature of things.

"Artworks have been turning to be mainly concerning ... themselves, as Earthly subjects and aspirations were abandoned decades ago, replaced with ... you know, fragmented colors of Cézanne, shapes of Kandinsky, lines of Mondrian?"

And an eighth (and final, promise) remembrance: my life is a perfume and my actions are volatile compounds that intermingle and enter into reactions with adjoining principles, engaging with the surrounding maze of chemical crosstalk, in ways that can be analyzed with impressive precision yet conversely are not predictable nor entirely understandable. Which is, I suppose, to say something about the inscrutable nature of Life and living, and the symptomatic difficulty of philosophers to formulate resonant explanations.

"The contemporary artist is on a tall building ledge threatening suicide, however he's more probably summoning attention, despairing yet unsure, the audience below mostly baiting him to jump, while a few try to spread out a net."

The conception of a life as a perfume also brings to mind that fragrance, by reason of its interwoven heritage and trademark suite of attributes, mirrors Life, more than any other currency of information or energy, any other medium of communication or potential form of art.

"Thomas Lawson grieved over art's inability to stimulate the growth of a troubling doubt."

Keeping on focus we notice … that, on the one hand, we're able to near-precisely elucidate the physico-chemical structures and properties of Nature's perfumes while, on the other, they're so idiosyncratically tangled as to render impossible any manner of systematic charting or mapping that makes evident sense. Moreover, we percipients are lexically frustrated to depict our experiences of these riddling cocktails of messenger metabolites.

"The perplexity, we imagine, is on account of the combinations of combinations of wave vibrations, if not some supplemental creditable perceptual mechanism."

So, without a good means of olfactive description, we're reminded of our position, in a way a contradiction, or more like a paradox, in that we rely on synesthetic metaphor, lexical loans from wordbooks of other senses, or alternatively by associating vaporous aromas with reminiscences, or by identifying their emanating sources.

"The feeling that we're feeling is not owing to our believing, to our holding that the scentful unfolding in Nature has meaning, that breathing around stands of conifer trees instills a moral calling, to defend the integrity of evergreen woodlands. Rather, it is owing to our perceiving, that is, owing to our sensory beholding."

This conversational salon may help us to make sense of our affiliation with alchemists, for we play the same secret seekers' game of reconciling different realms. It is by virtue of the agency of perfume as both corporeal substance and ethereal unseen, that it is uniquely poised to bridge or span the gap, to connect and bind realities.

"We are their rightful heirs? by carrying on with the alchemical program? which is not inconceivable to crack, as we've only to continue refining our interpretations."

A radical program in alchemy may be our business, like our home ground, given that the scientific community is in a blood oath with value-free technology.

"Dissolve and combine, *solve et coagula*, the volatilization of the fixed and fixation of the volatile, the materialization of fancy and dematerialization of form, the passing from one phase into another and back."

We see that academia has entered into a marriage of convenience with centers of power, that polity is drained dry of sincerity, media purged of any noble intentions, religion withering on the vine, all colluding on the global project to execute a radical makeover of Life.

"If pure objectivity were to become pure subjectivity, it could begin and end with fragrance. If a pure idea or a feeling were to become pure matter, it could begin and end with fragrance."

Perfumes of Pretense
(Bergamot)

"There is not a lot of high-mindedness in Nature. I'd say there is moral blindness. Yet curiously, there are random acts of kindness."

"Bergamot?"

Greetings, please be seated, as the proceedings are to be preceded, with an allegory worth repeating. Saffron will relate an exchange between a mystic and a scientist and a naturalist:

"I need to see it—says the lab-bench physicalist. To the contrary—argues the unswerving spiritualist. But the revering student of Nature, sitting on the ground under moonlight, spying with her infrared flashlight the behaviors of night-flying lepidopterans, she answers—you two, you both reduce the splendorous tree of Life, you the researching scientist by pruning variables, and you the meditating mystic, pruning by integration, you bedfellows both yearning for unification, with your inviolable laws, be they physical or immaterial. Why not the pair of you join me instead, in the mud, and watch the show of flitting hawkmoths, actors in this messy midnight drama?"

There isn't much fixed or absolute or universal in the Natural World, not oneness, instead there is one-of-a-kindness.

"Unbreakable laws reveal fissures, hard rules are exposed to have soft spots, lock-tight theories pop off rivets and develop leaks."

The budding naturalist, when investigating plant and animal communities, observes that common knowledge is usually wrong, and so turns to scientific literature, but finds published studies to be frequently misleading so turns to firsthand experience, then learns of the limits to empirical findings. With each humbling step, the apprentice in natural history is further initiated into the realm of enigmatic complexity, unfolding vitality, pluralism and inconsistency, chance and contingency, unforeseeable emergence, nuance and anomaly, elaboration and novelty, all characterizing continuously.

"Those revelations impart a deep engaging reverence for Creation or a dose of deferential awe, depending on the initiate's temperament."

You might say that the naturalist is naturally situated in that unoccupied area of inquiry, that no-man's land between the magisteria of Earth and ether, albeit dwelling more in the former than the latter.

"The path of the natural historian cuts deeply sometimes, yet the field of vision is broad most of the time, with Living Nature central in our sites."

The naturalist assumes residence where paradoxicalness appears to preside, and general principles are nudged aside, where properties are intricately measured but not all the time, where Nature reveals itself upon rigorous study but not totally, where material evidence is awarded great weight but not too much weight, where experiments disclose the nature of Life but don't divulge all.

"Bergamot?"

In seconds we detect a projection of lemons, then the introduction lessens, with splashes of lime and grapefruit also making our acquaintance among that early vaporescence.

"Lifting evocations of sparkling citrus and juicy berries assert a naturalistic tanginess—the dry bitter-orange complexion shortly yields to a cellulosic influence fronting floral back-notes—are we reviewing the same sample here? which is brisk and clean, crisp and green?—yes, but an unambiguous estery effect is reflected, reminiscent of clary or lavender—I'm blown away by how tones of rosewood and damp herbs are blowing every which way."

The essential oil is drawn from Nature by means of mechanical cold expression, which entails rasping and centrifugal separation from tiny sunken glands within the outer layer (*flavedo*) of fresh peels of nearly ripe non-edible (the pulp is bitter and sour) fruits that grow on the diminutive bergamot trees cultivated in North Africa and Ivory Coast and mostly (up to ninety percent) on the Calabrian coast of southern Italy, where there is long experience of the centuries-old tradition.

"We regard the oily entity, the flowery framework, the bed of balsamic character—in comparison to other citrus zest oils, the constellation of heart-notes is more richly nuanced and busy—the suave herbal harmony makes a unique feature for sure—much as it may be a circular association, there is no mistaking the insinuating or flat-out indicating of Earl Grey tea?—and for all the tingly bracing and lively effusing, the fluid perfume is deeply resonant and rounded as well—do I alone make out an olfactive nod to galbanum?—but you notice the floating leafy lemon-pepper reference? the layered vegetational presence? in the, errr, the later section let off from the essence?"

The fragrance family known as *chypre* comprises a model triad of volatile oils of which bergamot is one, alongside oakmoss and labdanum. The three in some way are joined, perhaps by a common resinous aspect? in any case, the individual oils are aesthetically linked, and constitute when all together a quality distinct. So the emergent combination has come to serve as a structural template, a blending strategy for composing a certain style of broad accord, inspiring thousands of variant fragrances, including some of the most notoriously noxious commercial successes (that's the extent of history we'll cover today).

"Our scentful expression from Ivory Coast is like a tribute to mandarin in the manner that it radiantly transmits a heavy cluttered chord remindful of that citrus species. The Italian in comparison is a tad soapy, bringing to mind a tobacco aroma with a suspended shade of tea making its way in the drydown bouquet."

In the matter of chemical components, there are quite a number of metabolic assertions: the ester linalyl acetate (elicits a sense of lavender), which is considered a marker of quality oils, is often well represented, its fraction benefiting by hot dry summers, thus fluctuating over time. The monoterpene limonene (contributes a lemony accent), however, is found in relatively small proportions compared to other types of hesperidia, not so dominating as elsewhere among pressed citrus oils. Also, there is beta-pinene (gives a piney green impression) and gamma-terpinene (puts oily terpenes on exhibit) and 4-carvomenthenol (imbues an edgy peppery sensation) and geraniol (suggests rose wax). And not least among ingredients is the trusty constituent linalol (supplies a woody blossomy element).

"And with respect to unmanipulated oils, there is a concerning issue of safeness, namely that of furanocoumarin toxicity which isn't trivial. Specifically, our consideration bears on the photo-mutagenic compound 5-methoxypsoralen (bergaptene)."

It causes a serious rash (I can testify) called berloque dermatitis (with a firsthand account).

"It is for this reason that rectified perilous-principle-free renditions of bergamot oil are standard stock of brokers. Of course, the oils upon reduction are not the same ... never the same (thinner, more lemon-like, less complex)."

This aromadermatological caveat prompts us to sadly deliver the warning so familiar: that the elegant construction of Creation that goes by the label *bergamot* is routinely watered down and touched up, debased by too many methods to enumerate (yet agents of the mainstream Perfume Cartel think it's all very well). The intervening might be accomplished with lemon or orange or petitgrain or rosewood or acetylated ho oil or lemon terpenes or natural or synthetic linalol or linalyl acetate or who knows what (but perfumers aren't troubled, they just don't care).

"In trade literature, monkeying with a distillate is termed *sophisticating.*"

Beware beware, that you can't compare (of course you're aware) an industrial ware to a natural fare. Yet canny counterfeiters are always improving their techniques ... is it too technical to explain here that those flagrant fraudsters of fragrance are occasionally exposed by their brazen impatience? that bergamot adulteration has been brought to light by the identification of chiral isomer ratios? notably linalyl acetate and linalol enantiomers. The detection is possible because racemic (fifty-fifty) mixtures of isomeric molecules are characteristic of abiotic reproductions, but not the original productions of aboriginal Nature.

"Segueing now ... perhaps time affords us this opportunity to review some customary essential oil designations ... hearing no objections..."

First, there are *genuine and authentic* oils, which we should hope are derived of real-World botanical taxa and haven't been tampered with by brokers (certifying agencies including Demeter and Ecocert and Vidasana and N&P will check for manipulation such as extending and deterpenating, decolorizing and recolorizing). A second class, so-called *pure and natural* or *food grade* oils, are likely to be compounded frankensteinish chemical conglomerations, the components perhaps developed owing to biotech wizardry, maybe via fermentation by genetically designed yeast organisms with computer-generated DNA sequences, originating from anything alive really (extracted from intestinal secretions of hamsters, what?), nevertheless we should optimistically trust that they're not produced from fossil fuel feedstocks. Another category, *nature-identical* oils, convey their cynical message by their given appellation, the insult built into the name (which is premised on the corrupting idea that Creation spelled with an upper-case C and creation with a lower-case c may as well be synonymous). Next, the term *natural fragrance* connotes just a little less than nothing. And substances labeled *fragrance oils* are guaranteed to be engineered corruptions of Living Nature through and through. But guess what?—none of these are legal denominations anyway, so our confidence level sags some, oh well.

"Every blind date from the Natural World is potentially a crafty nature-identical seductress from the neighborhood."

No, the term *nature-identical* is not a joke. Yes, it's a contemptuous ploy. No, it won't set back our resistance to the desecrating program administered by the Chemical Industry. Yes, it's a sobering lexical introduction to the field of organic chemistry. No, we won't abide such inimical disregard for Creation and haughty hostility to Life.

"Have you come across this phrase?—*die Endlösung der Naturfrage*—that would be the final solution to the question of Nature?"

Perfumes of Subterfuge
(Bakul)

"Monarchs?"

We spot the butterflies outside, en route to their overwintering grounds down the road from here. They are fulfilling the terminal stretch of their southward migration, which by their numbers is less considerable than in the past, in part due to the decline of northern milkweed populations (thanks Monsanto, for your triumphant herbicide Roundup).

"Next is the latest of a continuing series, our salon preambulary reviews of Industry-darling perfumers, of the established and promising, the go-getting and up-and-coming," Saffron announces.

Say, when DDT was first introduced decades ago to California farms, who wondered about the concerning fate of pelican eggshells on Pacific Islands? A mighty few saw that stealthy sabotage coming? Did anyone at the time ask questions germane? whether the operating record of chemical pesticide purveyors was error-free? whether they had any interest in the welfare of plants? animals? soils? skies? seas? ecological communities?

"Much as it has been problematical to select just a single winner from among so many qualified—the finalists included notables such as Roucel, Polge and Demachy and Buxton, Ellena, Giacobetti and Tauer, Guillaume, Sieuzac and Sheldrake and Ménardo and Morillas—the decision has been reached: the annual award for the most hubristic chemical huckstering goes to … (drum roll)…"

Yet still, we consign our fortunes to the same abusive ilk, those with corporations like Monsanto, of course, but also affiliated agents of ideological alliances, for instance, functionaries of mass perfumery, the ecology-oblivious intention-ambiguous effectively promiscuous molecule-diddling deniers of mysterious … Life.

"Francis Kurkdjian is the winner. We presently recognize his odorful compositions, including *Iris Nobile* by Acqua di Parma, *Eau Noire* by Christian Dior, and *Le Mâle* by Jean Paul Gaultier."

Kurkdjian rants against the spirit of vitalism and analogizes that just like writers, who require access to entire vocabularies in order to make their arguments, perfumers need synthetic ingredients in order to aptly express themselves.

"His are busy contributions to epidemic endocrine disruption."

More than that, his introductions advance the wholesale disrupting of elements in Nature that are situationally nuanced, adaptively time-refined and refinedly designed, impenetrably involved and vital and vulnerable.

"The flea-powder facet and the liquorice and spoiled-curry aspects of his *Eau Noire* cologne are associated with dizziness and nausea, shortness of breath and chest pains… and probably reduced sperm counts."

More than that, his achievements are associated with widespread aesthetic atrophy and degradation of cultural landscapes, which happen to coincide with the disappearing from physical landscapes of various newts and violets, beetles and orchids and raptors, bees and columbines and marine mammals.

"Wilful blindness, never worsted by enlightened kindness, enables a kind of bloated boasting that's worse than mindless."

His sycophantic clientele seem pleased by his puffed-up notions of power and control and his practice absent guideposts, absent bearings, absent limits, absent testing, absent any constraints.

"Knowledge of natural history invites a sense of the sacredness of Creation, revealed as particular and unfolding."

Perfumes of the Natural World instead are emissary expressions of metabolic life, formed and tested over ages and ages, with myriad organic accords fitted to dynamic ecologies, of a certain quality and a certain quantity but without a certain rationale, in a certain order at a certain time and a certain place but without a certain purpose, yet with a certain congruous presence and a certain Earthly integrity.

"The term *emissary* is derived from the Latin *emittere,* meaning to send out, as in emit, as in emission, as in volatile emission, as in perfume."

"We are now suddenly traveling to Indian shrines and festivals? experiencing the exalting vapors wafting from garlands woven of bakul flowers offered for *pooja?*"

In the matter of today's aromatic study, which we admit is promotional, but as always, much more than notional: first off, we're surprised that the Indian flower oil, which is known as bakul, is little known, that the alluringly elegant extractive material familiar to us is unfamiliar to most.

"A syrupy suggestion a caramelic complexion a smooth structure a creamy character a honeyed heart a floral focus a deep drydown a persistent personality an aztec goddess dipping her hair in jars of melted *piloncillo*."

More than tropical, the fragrance seems delicate and ethereal, radiating and then turning immaterial. Such evanescent demeanor is unusual for a sphingophilous blossom, though the rich parcels of infochemicals set loose are coincidingly heavy and heady as we'd expect of molecular invitations dispatched to moths who get busy after sunset.

"Perhaps *Mimusops elengi* could benefit from better-focused public relations? as the tree's standing has been spread thin, across a slew of different denominative epithets, going colloquially by Spanish cherry, maulsari, Asian bullet wood, bakula, West India medlar, and a good number more, as well as various appellations in Hindi and Sanskrit and other languages."

All the same, we've always regarded the plant extract as bakul.

Perfumes of Furtiveness

I remind Saffron not to forget to get out the *mouillettes* as she sets up the lesson in preparation.

The question I'm guessing you're asking is why she's setting up to set out with a session of a succession of volatile expressions?

"So then, it's true that the biota dwelling on our skin are fond of epidermal flakes?" arriving guests anticipate the theme of tonight's gathering.

Whereas we think of the term *muskiness* as denoting the fragrant character of certain materials of the perfumer's palette, this attributive, *musky,* which we assign to describe the nutty pungent buttery animalic sweet sensory aspect (alluring to many crepuscular moths and bats ... and preferred by formulators to aromatize laundry detergents?), is also depictive of the elicitative cocktail of steroidal compounds produced by microbes metabolizing apocrine secretions around hairy labyrinths of human loins and especially underarms.

"Those bodily sites facilitate odorful infochemical flights," Saffron says.

Since those sheltered body regions are so positively suited for microscopic creatures to live and lodge and perform their work, with all the surface area for wicking and launching, they're like

semaphores of scent, conducive to the production and disper-
sion of messaging metabolites.

"A courtship attractant in that brew, found elsewhere in
Nature too, happens to be at issue: androstenol is a wee con-
troversial, being a purported human-male chemical come-on."

Yet that steroid is not of single (hominid-armpit) origin, but
is the very same pig saliva component so notable for its pheromonal swine-seducing sway, and is produced and discharged
also by fungi such as truffles.

"Still, we agree, that the term muskiness olfactively character-
izes people's pee?"

On account that many of the compounds at issue, that the
emissive subjects of our inquiry also pass with urine, the perfume
of this fluid waste material is judged to be musky. Also, urinous
odors are considered steroidal because there are metabolites
within the yellow ammoniacal stream that are breakdown products carrying indicators of sexual condition.

"Meanwhile, our underarms turn out aromatic references to
cows and goats, truffles and pigs and fish, eesh."

Axillary diffusers most prevail upon us, claiming our attention as they host the effusive liftoff of evaporating molecules so
rousingly acrid and perhaps hircine, even rancid by the microbial
metabolism of sebum to short-chain fatty acids.

"And something more is connoted, like charred hamburger?"

Heavier substances of greater mass are modified by the unseen
activity of microorganisms to yield compounds of low molecular
weight that provide burnt notes. And the distinction of fishiness
is principally perceived upon the ascent of nitrogenous perfumes
issued from female genitals during special observances, including though not limited to semen lingering around the vagina.

"Much as the scent of foreskin secretions is comparable, we sense your uneasiness to call it cheesy? as if this cheesiness makes you queasy? and your queasiness sure comes easy."

Well, that's not my area of expertise.

"And elements extricating from the ecosystems of our scalps?"

The chemical couriers set loose for dissemination from head hair are principles nurtured by sweat, which reveal muted tones and lactonic chords, peachy coconut nuances and expressions of crumbled cheese sprinkled around due to yeasts incubating.

"And morning breath?"

Propelling fumes of exhalation are contrastingly like malodorous projectile weapons issued by bacterial metabolism of saliva, sometimes comprising volatiles of indole and skatole, sometimes sulfurous, sometimes steroidal, sometimes just like garlic oil, which provokes us to recoil.

"And sweaty feet?"

Armies of microbes work to supply sulfur-containing molecules for distribution among vapors that emanate from feet, which have been cut off from exposure to circulating air.

"And the transmission of fecal odors, you know?"

I've heard.

"Of our antecedents, the anus was an unavoidable part of genital inspection, which is to say that there's an erogenic suggestiveness owing to a genetic retentiveness bearing merely on body location."

Perfumes of Progress
(Wöhler)

1828—Look, Mom, no kidneys needed—who doesn't recognize this historic declaration?

"I can make urea without calling on my kidneys," Saffron recites the actual quote.

In any case, the story on record is that Friedrich Wöhler deals the vital-force theory a fatal blow by demonstrating that there is no mystery to organic substances, thus disproving the notion that unknowable forces in organisms make life possible. That's the official account, that Wöhler's experiment upsets the theory of vitalism. So now, humankind won't be held back from cooking up any chemical compound under the sun.

"Of course, we don't buy it, the great lie of physicalism."

This is to say that we've come to a critical juncture along our time-line, at which point Wöhler resumes his offensive against biological exceptionalism. First he made oxalic acid, now he's making urea. This time he really does it, scoring big, obscuring the distinction between organic and inorganic, eagerly blurring that line.

"Of course, we're not going along with the reduction of breathing beings to inert chemicals."

The celebrated event transpires on a routine day in February … Wöhler heats up ammonium cyanate, expecting only to liberate some cyanide, but instead is left with crystals of urea, which happens to be the same metabolite concentrated in our urine.

"Of course, we would never agree that Living Nature is, in essence, dead matter and energy in space."

Wöhler's synthesis suggests that organic substances, such as sugars and alcohols, known of living organisms, can be prepared from non-living materials. The implications of this are understandably disconcerting to vitalists, who defend the sacrosanct status of all Life.

"High-flown mystical conceptions of what it means to be alive, owing to Wöhler's fateful find, appear now to be belied."

The discovery looks to be at variance with the vitalistic idea that mechanistic models are not by themselves sufficient to explain living processes. And so, conquistadors in Chemistry are congratulating themselves for invalidating our deep intuition that Earthly Life comprises more than the scrutable sum of inert physical and chemical and energetic components. Vitalism, we have no choice but to admit, has been dealt a significant blow, and is presently on the retreat.

"The depreciators of Life, who scoff at the mystery of living, with an early streak of determined binging to knock off Nature, they are just beginning. And as it turns out, they'll never stop."

Yet, a fact remains that is scarcely addressed: organic compounds in their nature bear out the meaning of the term … *inimitable*. And the organic tissues that they constitute are an order more distinguishably involving. The new scientific consensus rules that nothing supernatural is at work—all right, fine. And the exceeding chemical complexity of living substances

will soon be widely attributed to the capacity of multiple carbon atoms to bond together—okay, sure. And this novel biotic
elaborateness and associated chemical behavior will be advanced
to justify the measureless patterns of fluxing variousness in
Nature—mighty straightforward.

"For all that, physicalists have not had the final word."

Is the benign synthesis of a small amount of urea truly such
a fatal setback for vitalism? still and all no, we don't think so.
Territory has been surrendered all right, defensive outposts
breached, but the new frontline trenches, we'll see, are where
they should have been all the while—defending the sanctity of
irreplaceable organic beings among countless unfolding biological economies, in this way defending the immensely entangled
ecologies of Life in continuous development for billions of years
to the point of impenetrable intricacy.

"Vitalism is the unambiguous affirmation of the goodness
of Creation, where gardens are associated with Eden and other
names for paradise," Saffron has memorized the poetic argu-
ment of Paul Lee? who doesn't shy from the moral dimension
of the matter.

"... and a defense of botanical and herbal gardens against the
experimental laboratory of modern science. After 1828, almost
everyone forsook the garden and botany and went into the lab.
They've yet to come out."

And Wöhler, however prideful and worked up, can also foretell
the hurt and damage in store. He remorsefully relates to a men-
tor that he'd witnessed the great tragedy of science: the slaying
of a beautiful hypothesis by an ugly fact (his words).

"No life force, nor any recondite influence from a mysterious
source, now stands in the way of the designs of humankind to

redesign and redefine and consign Life to an assembly line or some comparable kind of denial of the vital at this time. Only the limits of our ingenuity can impede the advancement at hand."

Wöhler's contribution to the grand program is both concrete and symbolic, on account that urea produced in a factory has critical implications for farming, as age-old traditions involving manure composting will soon be broken up by the introduction of industrial synthetic fertilizers. And soon too will surge other cases of intervening by humanity in Nature-honed cycles, and of the technological denial of limits in many spheres of life.

"The neomanic push will prove to be unbending, to replace the fine-tuned situational time-tested contingent expressions of the Natural World with unconditional fabrications of sapiens."

1832—The German poet botanist zoologist geologist physicist philosopher and ... professed vitalist ... becomes mortally ill.

"Johann Wolfgang von Goethe."

Some of his colleagues theorize that his death was a reaction to Wöhler's synthesis, given that he was surely aware of the deteriorating prospects for vitalism as an organizing influence in fields of inquiry and endeavor. For several decades he'd been providing commentary in the form of his running epic poem *Faust*, based upon the classic German legend concerning a man who sells his soul to the Devil in exchange for knowledge. Rest in peace, Goethe.

"It's starting, the symbolic commencement party in honor of the new campaign of biophobic boundlessness."

Perfumes of Indifference
(Magnolia)

The book of Life consists of sentences that nearly never were, and never will be again. This is at odds with that other book, the one cited by Galileo.

"The grand book of the universe is written in the language of mathematics. That book?"

That book over which we raise our right hands and swear to tell the truth, so-called. The book of recipes for success in these times. The how-to book on commerce and media, polity and religion, and love, which has excited among humanity such a massive following. Yes, that book. It has an instructional chapter about reduction, the program of practice called reductionism, how to break things up into constituent units united by their adherence to integrative principles, how to discard outliers. And a chapter about unifying patterns, constant and overarching. And another about ultimate meaning, and a section about time-lessness, and another about perfection, and one about absolute truth, and another about the *aum* sound of God.

"The book is continuously being reissued in a never-ending series of imprints. That book?"

And there's a chapter about extension and amplification, about connectivity and networks and the phenomenon of viral propagation across social media, and about the benefits generally of dealing with specificities in a general manner, about reaping influence by means of generality dressed up as particularity (which should particularly be a compulsory read for corporate executives concerned with global reach). Yes, that book.

"The book details why cosmological musing has become an endeavor that is so alluring? That book?"

The book's later editions have emphasized the future, covering the subjects of vicariousness and cybernetics in depth, with interactive chapters about new kinds of consciousness, and an addendum about the coming proliferation of mind cloning. And there's a summarizing chapter that addresses all different manner of virtuality and abstraction. Yes, that book.

"The book is written in the language of numbers? That language?"

The language by which two unique individuals plus two more unique individuals equals exactly four unique individuals, however the countless variables are wiped away in order to carry out the equation. Yes, that language. The language by which mystifying nuance is divided up and knotted arguments are dumbed down, unfathomable intricacy is streamlined and unforeseeable effects of causes are set aside, opaque contingent conditions are denied and unintelligible elaborateness is nullified. The language by which messy rough edges are planed to be flawlessly smooth. The language of all time and everywhere, of the infinitesimally small and inconceivably large, of the immutable and inevitable and everlasting, of chemical potentials and mass and motion, of quarks photons neutrons and wormholes, of cyborgs and prosthetics and brain emulation, of cyberspace and immortality. The one-size-fits-all language of physics and power and salvation. Yes, that language.

(Saffron has already begun passing around strips of blotter paper dipped in a yellowish oil.)

"Whereas the floral perfume staged by these lightweight metabolites, such as it obliquely elicits the ylang-ylang brand of nectareous floweriness, much as it reflects tuberose even less than that, connotes a minimum of cinnamon and a modicum of clove, as it effuses fairly fruity but not fruitcakey, not pulpy and not juicy, though drying away with more grass than hay, and in any event, the presently referenced scent summons more pasture than silage, just as the instillment is sweet as it is still a little tart."

Our sample, we trust it's authentic ... an essential oil from China, we're not entirely sure ... from a distillation of a solvent extract, supposedly ... we believe it's *Magnolia grandiflora*, the one and only ... southern magnolia...

"A vanilla undercurrent extends a lemony complexion which envelopes a gardenia core which is expanded upon by a lily-of-the-valley note which draws attention away from a creamy-while-still-resinous heartbeat which is exalted by a fresh-yet-not-green impression which is toned down by the vanilla undercurrent."

We have a problem.

"The problem is that magnolia is yet another of numerous perfumery materials skillfully compounded to satisfy in-the-family fancies having little to do with real plants."

The magnolia line of descent extends back more than a hundred million years, and the flowers are considered to be morphologically primitive based on their relatively unspecialized structures. The early diversification is indicated also by the sloppy pollinating arrangement forged with beetles, who feast orgiastically in the proteinaceous mess.

"We think that's called pollenamory."

"Is it an olfactive hallucination or do I sense a diffusive radiation like a perfumey drift of lavender? a sensation of esteric derivation due to the sensory action of a clary-like emanation? a scentful suasion of clary sage? and am I delirious to sense that this selection is in some fashion like an infusion of hot green tea with the addition of chocolate flakes?"

Blossoms of southern magnolia symbolize a love for life, according to readings of floriography, a discipline that lends meaning to types of flower arrangement.

"To some, magnolia blossoms stand for the genteel values of Jim Crow Mississippi, the magnolia state."

The scent of magnolias, sweet and fresh, then the sudden smell of burning flesh, a pastoral scene of the gallant South, the bulging eyes and the twisted mouth (it's from the Billie Holiday song "Strange Fruit"). In any event, we should note that these days one is less likely to happen upon a black man swinging by his neck from a magnolia tree.

"The perfume from Nature, to an extent, recalls honeysuckle, and is distantly reminiscent of cherry blossom, and resembles also orange flower, though the association is oblique. But really, magnolia is just like magnolia and nothing else but magnolia."

Headspace analyses reveal substantial fractions of the camphorous ketones isopinocamphone and verbenone, molecular findings that are difficult to figure, on account that the vaporous fragrancy lifting from flowers seems anything but ketonic? so we are left to throw up our hands and ascribe the puzzling profile as a curiously abstruse design of Creation.

"The *Magnolia* cologne by Demeter is promoted by its proprietor, Christopher Brosius, as taking you back to an old Southern plantation."

It is rumored that the catchphrase *I hate Life* has already been trademarked by Brosius to serve as a future brand name in anticipation of a more forthright business venture in perfumery (ja-ja). But seriously, he's considered a renegade of the contemporary perfume scene by virtue of the crafty contrariness of his marketing strategies? the creatively nonconforming way he positions his Earth-incongruous concentrates? those proxy perfumes that we find to be so insulting?—we who hold dear the fate of actual plant and animal species and communities, which he deems are his business to odorfully impersonate.

"Scent is life—that's what Brosius has trumpeted."

So, by adding a portion of oncidal from Dragoco, a helping of hedione and a tinge of trimenal and a pinch of florex from Firmenich, a handful of hasmigone from Bedoukian, a dose of dupical and a dab of sandela from Givaudan, a shot of liffarome and a spot of citralva and a fragment of vertofix from IFF, then a handful of isolates and duping compounds to impart complementary powdery floral woody green citrusy and fixing elements, and ... and *voilà*, we've constructed a gag-worthy chemical swipe at those vital beings most vulnerable in the World. We'll name the fragrance ... magnolia.

"It's the story of Life."

Perfumes of Elegy
(Bitter Almond)

Willkommen. As there is no panel review queued for this evening, we figured to address instead a query received regarding almond oil, the oily sort—no, it's not toxic, but the essential oil is another story, albeit everything in the marketplace is rectified. Shall we have a little talk about this?

"So, before there was Life on Earth, early appearing organic compounds were derived by condensation of hydrogen cyanide, a molecule that was to take on, a few billion years hence, quite a number of diverse duties," Saffron sets up the matter at hand.

Pardon me this unsettling yet pertinent excursus, concerning Jews who were transported by rail from Europe to Auschwitz-Birkenau in 1942.

Over several months, the thousands who arrived were initially herded onto a wooden *Judenrampe* for selection, those ticketed for death taken to a couple of remote converted farmhouses, referred to as the little red house (with brick walls) and the little white house (with plastered walls). These served as provisional chambers for extermination with hydrocyanic acid (hydrogen cyanide), presaging larger-scale operations to come.

In his diary, touching on the approach to these two dwellings, Höss the camp commandant described how men and women unsuspectingly walked to their death through an orchard of blossom-laden fruit trees.

"It appears that the two gassing bunkers were surrounded by wooded countryside consisting of poplar and birch stands, and in particular, drupaceous species (stone fruit trees) of the Rosaceae, which would have been in bloom that spring."

The two country cottages had signs on their doors that read *zum Baden* (to the baths). Their aging thatched roofs were propped up by wooden ceilings that were reinforced and made airtight. The windows were bricked over and had small swinging wood planks that sealed at the edges with felt. The floors were strewn with sawdust, as there was no plumbing and so no water to clean the messes.

"It appears that the victims passed under cherry and plum trees, which were broadcasting shares of various shikimate volatiles along with abundant low-molecular-weight terpenoid metabolites, including carotenoid degradation products. Some nitrogenous components were probably given off as well. And surely also, those familiar bitter-almond-toned principles: benzenoid aldehyde, aka benzaldehyde, prone to sway a given bouquet, issues a curiously similar heliotropin-like or soft hawthorne aroma as does hydrogen cyanide, though the olfactive character of the latter compound is slightly more ligneous and delicate."

Hydrogen cyanide in concentration is an effective fumigation agent used by people against lice and many other vermin. Historically known as prussic acid, the insecticide was marketed for use in death camps under the brand name Zyklon-B.

"So then ... that foreboding floral perfume, the distinguishing vaporous transmission wafting among those being marched to their murder, the fragrant sweet-and-creamy evocation of marzipan, slightly balsamic owing to the oxidation of benzaldehyde to yield esters of benzoic and cinnamic acids, foreshowed the chemical carnage impending."

Since there was no plumbing, gassing was carried out in the dark of night to minimize panicked yelling and attempts to escape by captives who might notice that the communal showers weren't actual showers. The Jews were told that they needed to undergo delousing, to undress and to remember the spot where they left their effects. Then they were directed, often with clubs and leashed police dogs, into one of the structures (as many as eight hundred at a time in the little white house and twelve hundred in the little red house).

"Fruits of trees assigned to the genus *Prunus* are termed *drupes*, characterized by a bone-hard pit of lignified endocarp tissue (inner ovary layer) enclosing a single seed. In this kernel's interior are cell vacuoles containing sequestered molecules of the cyanogenic glycoside, amygdalin, which is considered a phytoanticipin, a plant defensive compound in place, awaiting activation. The trigger in Nature would normally be tissue damage caused by some creature with a strong jaw and hard teeth and an appetite for seed cake."

Amygdalin, a bitter-tasting white crystalline chemical broker of life and death.

"In fruits, the glycosidically mediated biological security system at the ready relies on a coupling process: a detonating action—in Nature, it would usually be an invasive disturbance—brings the water-soluble amygdalin into contact with enzymes that catalyze a hydrolytic cleavage—in Nature, animal saliva would satisfy the reaction's requirement of water—yielding glucose and ... benzaldehyde and hydrogen cyanide, the associating perfume and perfumed poison, the metabolic twosome and olfactory tweedledee and tweedledum."

After the doors were bolted shut, gas-tight tins (with the *Giftgas* warning labels removed) containing the delivery system of small pellets of impregnated silica gel were opened, and the Zyklon-B poured into the wall hatches, upon which the lethal vapors along with the ethereal fragrancy of cherry amaretto would radiate.

"This substance, amygdalin, lurks in the tissues of quite a number of plants. It is found only as traces in domesticated sweet almonds, whereas the bitter variety and wild forms harbor more substantial amounts, so consequently those are potentially toxic and their sale restricted in the United States. Yet the barred nuts are still procured (apricot kernels similarly) from various purveyors like health food stores, for unsanctioned medicinal and culinary applications, such as the tradition-faithful preparation of marzipan. (The recipe passed down has us grind into a paste ninety-nine percent sweet with a smidgen of aromatic bitter almonds. We're instructed not to worry over any peril of poison as the tiny fraction of hydrocyanic acid in the doughy confection becomes negligible by its exposure to air. Of course, the widely available inauthentic rendition today is flavored instead with synthetic benzaldehyde.)"

After a few minutes of screaming and seizures and retching, when the commotion died down, an SS man wearing a gas mask would review the scene through a peephole. (Early attempts were bungled miscalculations, but eventually, after several messy trials, the optimal amount of prussic acid was administered.) The *Sonderkommando* cleaned the chambers of blood and excrement, but would first need to disentangle the bluish or pink-hued bodies, which were often clinging to each other, half-squatting as there was no space to fall down. Sometimes there was green or yellowish frothy bile smeared and dripping all over the place. Then they loaded the dead onto carts and dumped them into nearby long burial pits near pine trees.

"Bitter-almond essential oil is obtained by means of steam distillation of press cake remaining after water maceration of the partially deoleated seeds, often from other *Prunus* like peach or plum or apricot. Of the distillate, the larger proportion of hydrocyanic acid is contained within the *hydrolat,* or hydrosol, which is the watery portion. Nonetheless, even ten drops of the potent metabolite can induce convulsions if ingested, so the five percent or less lurking in the volatile oil renders it dangerously toxic. The old labels FFPA (free from prussic acid) would indicate that hydrogen cyanide had been removed by treatment with calcium hydroxide and ferrous sulphate."

Later, on account that they were contaminating the ground water, the putrefying corpses in the mass graves were exhumed and incinerated on pyres. And the two farmhouses became converted again, this time to be used as undressing rooms for those who would subsequently be shot and hurled immediately thereafter onto the flames, often while still alive.

"These days bitter-almond oil is more frequently concocted from a petroleum precursor like toluene. The FFC (free from chlorine) label is a sure indication of such synthesis. And much as it is widely considered a mono-component oil, like wintergreen (composed of methyl salicylate) or ho leaf (of linalol), a genuine bitter-almond oil that reflects chemical profiles of actual wild plants is not purely benzaldehyde—no way—not at all, err, not all of it—there are other molecules contained, even if only in traces."

Adolf Hitler and Eva Braun died by taking pills of hydrogen cyanide. Those who later handled their bodies reported an odor of bitter almonds.

Perfumes of Prejudice

"I'm brainstorming, developing postmodern flavor profiles, part of a concept for a new highly evolved cuisine, creating expressions of flat moldy acrid skunky tallowy sawdust, get the idea? mouth-puckering rotten-eggy tarry choking urinous gasoline, how about it? sour lactic sulphury melted-rubber burned-bakelite and sickly acetous cabbage, can't fail right?"

(Saffron, referring to my nervousness about the disturbances at the *perfumería,* says that the recurring stirrings aren't disturbing.)

No, I take little notice of the trucks over there, with the bumper stickers displaying the Ferrari logos, nor do I keep tabs on all the coming and going, which you say is owing to nothing worth knowing, nor do I presume anything about the collection of tools stashed behind the boxes of *eau de parfum,* around the mound of cases of *Lovely* by Sarah Jessica Parker, in back of the stack of *L'Eau d'Issey* by Issey Miyake, odd appliances of the sort that can be used to administer electric shocks, implements that have been confiscated from narco hideouts.

(Saffron says that I always imagine the worst, that the recurring disturbances at the *perfumería* shouldn't be stirring up any nervousness.)

"No one is impressed anymore by a Colt pistol with a gold grip. It's practically standard-issue on the street. And the cock-fights are unsettling bloody contests, true, but nothing sinister is at work. There is gambling, of course."

(Saffron says I shouldn't be worrying over any stirrings there, or anything concerning the *perfumería*, which I find disconcerting.)

They host rollicking Christmas parties I've heard.

"You get carried away. They bend a law now and then, vouch-safe for a couple of unlicensed nightclubs, that's all."

So I shouldn't draw any conclusions from those ostrich-skin boots that your admirer flaunts?

"That's the old-school style of *narco cultura*, which doesn't mean anything. The *comandante* is just a friend, by the way, a regular guy with average interests, same diversions and dreams as anyone. You should check out his stockpile of DVD's. He even hosts his own fun website."

I've noticed that most narcos have their own social-media pages. They upload pics of themselves showing their faces blood-ied and hands with fingers missing.

"So what do you think? about a cutting-edge restaurant serving up yeasty fishy fecal cheesy solvent-soaked vomitous overcooked greens, safe bet, no? dirty rusty tinny musty catty ammoniacal machine-oil-filled can liner, sure to be popular, what? gassy tannic meaty carbolic musky hircine smoky sewer drain, certain success, you know it?"

Perfumes of Promise
(Hydrosols)

✦

Saffron announces, "*Hydrolats*, the byproduct waters of distillation, condensed from steam, are not our primary focus, nevertheless we don't mind a short respite to accept and accession this engaging shipment just arrived?—"

Science (inflaming) has failed Life.

"...of larch a fresh-resinous after-bathing stimulating body splash, and cineolic lavender to calm air-travel jitters and skin rashes, and neroli diluted is quite helpful with hysterical children—"

Religion (withdrawing) has failed Life.

"...and juniper berry a lively astringent spray for vibrational work and to drink for internal cleansing, and clove-breathing bay leaf a complete lymphatic-system cleansing program—"

The money economy (inundating) has failed Life.

"...and thyme with savory a gripping antiseptic mouth rinse, and tarragon an antispasmodic artemisia for coaxing digestive juices, functionally best to group with culinary umbellifers—"

Art (sublimating) has failed Life.

"…and radiant verbena water a substitute for the costly essential oil to allay mental disturbances, and tea tree for disinfecting scrapes and sores and mouth cankers, and sage with a sprig of spearmint makes an herby summer toddy—"

Polity (exploiting) has failed Life.

"…and rosemary verbenone effective for terpene-mediated respiratory treatment, and rose an exalting emotional rescue, and peppermint to relieve colitis and itches, and scotch pine an immune system accelerator—"

Music (palliating) has failed Life.

"…and green myrtle a mucolytic agent, plus useful in concert with cornflower to rescue irritated eyes, and melissa for hot flashes a floral alternative to the pricey oil, and oregano a germicidal tonic remember to dilute, and basil for menstrual cramping—"

Philosophy (abstracting) has failed Life.

"…and blue spruce a dry pine-foresty headnote our preferred choice for adrenals, spray liberally to the kidney area, and geranium mmm aromatically resplendent, balancing for facial skincare—"

Humanity (devouring) has failed Life.

So without delay, we turn from representations, from the negation of Creation by the promiscuous crusaders and disconnected mediators and administrators of unconditional and non-contextual counterfeit conventions, from disregardful surrogates and sponsors of inert offerings, to Life on its own terms, by its first-chosen and prevailing currency of communication…

Perfumes of Dissent
(Terroir)

On every continent, in every place of worship, in every institution of higher learning, in every legislative chamber, in every war room, in every arena of life, in every aspect of culture, at every turn, it's happening.

"This evening, the scheduled salon has been canned in favor of another just planned, a lineup of tastings not tidings, sipping not dipping, concerning a confirming however disturbing interpretation from the world of wine, vinous testimony apprising that the siege—"

The siege has been laid to Life.

"In no particular order, the first mystery flight issues on the *nariz* welcome wisps of starfruit and stewed apple—some mid-palate lardy lanolin and papaya-pulp vapors dance around the pharynx—there's a sense of combusting firewood volatiles, the dispersing barbecue smoke produced from spruce, succeeded by a secondary scentful sensation of smoothly skirting guava or goji berries—a boiled nearly rotten beetroot bottom is suspended in the extended fragrant fading finish."

Veteran *vignerons* with small plots of grape vines across countrysides of France and Italy warn of the groundswell, their field of endeavor increasingly carried away by consumer capitalism and flattened out by the blunt sledgehammer of mass opinion, stylized and conventionalized with vinicultural technologies like reverse osmosis and cryoextraction, and microoxygenation, which they liken to botox, and aging in oak *barriques,* which they compare to plastic surgery or worse. Electroconvulsive therapy, for example, has been raised as an analogy on account that the wine is imbued by obscuring vanillin, which narrows ranges of nuance and dulls personality, which masks identifying quirks and distinctions of character in such a way that the *terroir* is snuffed out and the wine, once singularly expressive of Life, loses its vital soul. It is dead (*le vin est mort*).

"The consultants say that they can't wait to begin growing grapes on the moon."

That's a rejoinder by advocates of empire. Mondavi, the beloved conquistador of monolithic thinking, also hopes to witness his heirs producing wines on other planets.

"New wine isn't put into old bottles. Those vessels used previously are shattered. Old societies collapse upon contact with the new," Saffron is translating from a French publication on the subject.

It's a head-on assault against the idea of *terroir*, the ideal of *terroir*, the notion of somewhereness, the expression of place, a specific point in space, the interplay of Earth earth vine and weather, soil drainage depth and texture, slope of the land, length of the days, and angles of the sun's rays. The advocates are resistance fighters, partisans up against it, pressured to get with the plan, like small grocers when mammoth supermarkets roll in, pushing back against phantoms of progress, against the steamrolling power of imperial dominion. They are unapologetic defenders of the *terroir*, champions of the *terroir*, fighting for values and livelihoods, making wines in the image of the *terroir*, serving the *terroir*. They explain that first one must discover the *terroir*, then find a way to express the *terroir*, which can take many generations. The region of Burgundy, for instance, where collective memory is long and strong, is one of their strongholds. The modernists call the unyielding old-timers peasants or hicks, or *terroir* terrorists.

"For a maximal impartment of vanilla aroma, the favored wine-racking barrels are constructed of hundred-plus-year-old French new oak trees hand-split into staves, which are then dried for several years, then toasted, the smaller the newer the better to conceal the wine's undressed nature with molecules of vanillin."

I think of auto-tuning, to cover up imperfections of pitch when vocalists sing out of tune, or Photoshopping, to manipulate images of fashion models.

"The subject of vanillization, that vanillic evocation, is principally due to the perfume of vanillin."

Vanillin is a single compound that leaches out from wood lignin of oak barrels, a process not unlike that by which vanilla metabolites from the vanilla fruit are extracted with aqueous alcohol to make the ethanolic tincture.

"All the same, we should point out that industrial vanilla materials, same as wine, are commonly constituted of vanillin from lignin, and nothing but, having nothing to do with vanilla the orchid."

It is owing to pied-piper Robert Parker and his hundred-point scale that selections placing high on scorecards are so frequently judged to be high-extract big-impression high-concentration big-experience high-and-big-everything with oak-woody intensity and that ubiquitous vanilla overlay, fulfilling the criteria that so many actors and agents in the world of wine have been in recent decades scrapping to emulate, effectively assigning their brands to the bandwagon of Parkerized wines.

"This next is a special drinking vintage by the way it asserts an ample oak-influenced Chablis-like astringent accord—emerges straight away with some summoning of cloves and a tribute to banana peel on a lactic bed of cottage cheese—plus a non-showy shade of cracked-graininess influences the mouthfeel? as though my cheeks are filled with chalky eggshells? the palate perhaps enveloped by flinty minerals?—finally we find a fizzy spritz of lemon rind, finely trailing among the sparkly tailing."

The appeal of authenticity in wine is the appeal of *terroir*, which is an appeal to something outside the self, be that a higher authority or a vulnerable ecology, and an appeal to something before the self, to history and heritage, context and continuity, and something after the self, to ongoing stewardship of place—

"Lifting from the glass's rim to bear early on the nares are inviting tidings of inky-black raspberries and canned peaches—there's a nice note which connotes a slice of spiced cinnamon toast which then turns to chewy raisin bread—also exhibits coumarinic midsection materializations which recall milfoil or woodruff or cut grass—and a minty element inside a rustic cedar box soaked in cough syrup?—the length is lasting by its lingering with flourishes of tamarind and cantaloupe and mocha."

…it's an appeal to the production of wine in broad totality by understanding environmental patterns and circumstances, natural settings and conditions, frames of reference and connections, as opposed to compartmentalizing and concentrating on manipulative practices based on specialized and insulated knowledge—

"A supple muscat-like indication shows on the initial nose, a convoluted chord of terpenes evoking watermelons and plummy cherries—transitioning to a warmed fruitcake, then maybe a mellow mango, then pizza dough, then Chinese dumplings—by deep breathing it gives a steely feeling? as if there's a secondary focus? of bell pepper dusted with Mexican chocolate?—then the balm continues on with a balanced *sobremesa*, a term that denotes a finish, this consisting of backnotes that reflect dried weeds and leather-strap principles."

…it's an appeal to honor traditional winemakers, their needs and aptitudes and interests, their poetic sympathies and aesthetic affinities, as we acknowledge the wreckful sources of their new fears, those mercenary technical directors who threaten to replace them, along with the ensuing practices of impersonal rubber-stamping based on external demands—

"Opening with an outpouring of youthful dandelion on the proboscis then followed by an olfactory trajectory of celery then seaweed then soon later veering to a rampant gamey redolence of venison and charcoal which surrounds or perhaps intertwines with a poised interior traction of yeasty pancake batter and maillard-toned chestnuts which yields to a presence that reveals on the latter palate as a vegetal facet of burnt eggplant with asparagus then shifting to a persisting bouquet which presides over the subdued fadeaway with decomposing fruit in a wet scrap bin."

...it's a love for time-weathered specificity rather than the seduction of unseasoned generality, for individual inimitable wines of distinct vintage and region rather than disembedded commodities scientifically proven to be the best, of situational idiosyncrasy rather than standardized uniformity, of natural satisfactions rather than products pointedly engineered to produce profits—

"Variation is real and concrete, variousness a fundamental condition of concrete reality, in contrast with the integrative ideas that go by terms such as *average* or *median*, *mode* or *norm*, late-arriving formulations of the human forebrain."

...these appeals are made with an awareness of limits to knowledge and uncertainty of outcomes, and an ability to spot blind technophilia wherever it rears its biophobic head, as in the case of predictable repeatable insurable oenological results based on viticulture manuals and viniculture databases and consulting-firm wine scores from mathematical algorithms and chemical analyses—

"We should skip this next selection, which is sticky and flat (and we liken to something dragged in by a cat), candy-coated and flabby (like something laid down by a tabby)."

...and made with a desire to illuminate and explore the diverse interplay of vine tending and grape growing and wine making and tasting, rather than chase a score with the aid of chromatography and mass-spectrometry to derive computerized quality indices—

"Whereas the concept of central tendency dwells in the town of abstraction that's in the state of reduction that's in the world of calculation, it has no place and is irrelevant in the World of Creation as it has materially existed for billions of years."

…it's an appeal to personalized solutions rather than universal fixes, to things that develop slowly through experience rather than immediately by design, to somewhere at some time rather than anywhere at any time, to the Nature-expressive for better or worse rather than the people-impressive by financial necessity or ideological obligation. It's an appeal to something we can't really own, whose purpose we can't fully apprehend, instead of some property of scaled production under off-site control by anonymous stakeholders—

"The nail that sticks out is beaten down."

These aggressive modernists don't affiliate with Life, and so they don't get it, don't care to catch on, don't care to listen, never studied living systems or natural history or any such field of inquiry, never paid much attention, and by extension don't consider that novelty and irreversibility are primary defining aspects of Nature, so they don't fret over the loss of unique bio-cultural expressions, aren't troubled or even concerned, figure general rules of the game won't disappear, elementary particles won't disappear, arithmetic won't disappear, their secure investments won't disappear, electronics won't disappear, God won't disappear, things they're comfortable with, that they align with, against the interests of the vital and vulnerable, irreplaceable cultures and communities of animals plants and people barely hanging on.

"They know what they're doing."

Perfumes of Transience

Incidentally, I've just read another one of these online articles by some son of a mother who is hosting or at least posting on one or another of these Internet websites, the kind where you find one tech lover after another rationalize his fashionable turning away from Creation in favor of the welcoming hideaway of abstract virtuality. The author says he had previously experimented with drugs and spiritualism (foreplay of estranging before engaging in the raging wide-ranging gangbang of materialism). These geeky humanists, as children they knew better, playing in dirt among plants and critters, building things with sticks and rocks. Then … the world of detached stargazers had its way with them? So, at some point this author left the garden for the media and meditation rooms and never looked back.

"All right then, next we assign homework, no kidding."

We translate and interpret, from the native tongue of Life.

Terms in French that we regularly employ—*parfum, chypré, soliflore, alambic, poudré, baume, parfumeur, mouillette*—learn these.

Certain words are taxing to fully grasp, so they may induce your brain to hurt—fatty, aminic, mossy, butyric, powdery, ozonic, crystalline, ketonic—master these.

Other designations provoke blank stares—naphthenic, norm-osmic, farinaceous, parosmic, tumaceous, phantosmic—memo-rize these.

Some can go one way or the other—nectarous or nectare-ous, hesperidic or hesperideous, camphorous or camphoraceous, vinous or vinaceous, umbelliferous or apiaceous, urinic or urin-ous—decide for yourselves, be consistent.

Expressions that have a nice collective ring?—anthranilic, vanillic, aliphatic, cresylic—balsamic, cineolic, borneolic, phe-nolic—become acquainted with these.

"Animalic, caramelic, aldehydic, pyrazinic, linalolic, terpenic, thujonic, agrestic?" Saffron adds.

Those too. And myrtaceous, liliaceous, sulphurous, rosaceous, mellifluous, tenacious, thuriferous, herbaceous, coniferous, malvaceous.

"Lactonic, solanaceous, thymolic, violaceous, fencholic, laura-ceous, anisic, apocynaceous, perfumistic, mephitic, coumarinic, rutaceous, lavandaceous, papilionaceous..."

So, Tulíp has returned from Cambodia?

"Yes, we talked ... about relationships. She said that you've not tried to contact her in over three years? and shared some intricacies that you've not previously revealed ... said you would hold forth concerning the grandness of silence yet in practice you cultivated only turbulence (her words)."

(Tulíp and I were never really in a relationship.)

"I invited her to join us."

(I'll take that as my cue to reveal, in the interest of providing a frame of reference, some expository details about the prin-cipal characters of this writing. I plan to cover the experiences of Tulíp, referring to her stay in Cambodia, where she learned all about the fragrant natural material aloeswood. And also those of Licorice, referring to her travels in Sierra Leone, where she gained expertise on another plant aromatic, karo-karounde. Their expeditions, I gather, were rewarding but not really figurative as we initially conceived. The original premise—solely my inspiration, they say, but that's not what I remember—was to seek out, from remote locations in Nature, perfumes of Creation wondrous to the highest degree, sensory indications of beauty and meaning so undeniable that they would serve as rallying points. The journeys, I understand, turned out to be rich with concrete revelation and poetic imagery, but not as I projected, not the way I imagined.)

The Perfume of Life is to be continued.

www.ingramcontent.com/pod-product-compliance
Lightning Source LLC
Chambersburg PA
CBHW032121020426
42334CB00016B/1028